HENRY IRWIN
AND THE
INDO SARACENIC
MOVEMENT RECONSIDERED

HENRY IRWIN
AND THE
INDO SARACENIC
MOVEMENT RECONSIDERED

PRADIP KUMAR DAS

PARTRIDGE
A Penguin Random House Company

To order additional copies of this book, contact
Partridge India
000 800 10062 62
orders.india@partridgepublishing.com

www.partridgepublishing.com/india

TO

AMITA

CONTENTS

LIST OF ILLUSTRATIONS

AUTHOR'S NOTE & ACKNOWLEDGEMENTS

I first set eyes on an Indo Saracenic building way back in 1967 during a professional visit to Madras (Chennai). The architecture was very different from where I came–Calcutta (Kolkata)–and I had difficulty relating to it. It seemed to me at the time, a curious concoction of Moorish, European and Islamic elements, which sat uncomfortably on each other and did not really belong to this country. I had not, at that point, appreciated that Indo Saracenic architecture was part of a 19th century British movement intended to project themselves as natural successors to the Mughals. Its principal protagonists were British engineers/architects in Southern and Western India. The Chennai skyline is dotted with buildings of this type and there were, and still are, a lot of people in South India who rightly think Indo Saracenic architecture is part of our heritage and should be preserved. As a first time visitor to the city, I had expected to see a lot more of the Georgian and Palladian type facades that one normally associates with Colonial architecture in South and South East Asia. As to the aesthetics of the new hybrid style, there are differences of opinion, just as there are many people who like "Rock" music or the paintings of Salvadore Dali or Mark Chagall because they are different. Others would not necessarily call them pleasing to the ear or beautiful. I tried not to be judgemental. Many years later, reading an article by Julian Baginni, an adviser on the Commission for Architecture and the Built Environment (CABE) I started to think about judgements of taste. Baginni held that "beautiful" is not the only positive aesthetic judgement and that there are other criteria. So too, a monument which constitutes a standard of public aesthetics may leave others cold. Much modern building in India tends to impact on space and some would agree that these are neither imaginative nor original. Others would argue that these buildings create or preserve spaces that enhance the lives of people who live in or use them. The ensuing pages examine some of these issues besides the story of a movement which led to a countrywide debate about its suitability to the Imperial ethos and the part played in that movement by individuals like Henry Irwin. Indo Saracenic architecture, a style heavily influenced by political considerations, was finally abandoned at the turn of the century. The subject was largely unfamiliar and the prospect of exploring a new field of rapidly advancing architectural history was fascinating.

Good or bad, ugly or beautiful, I think a lot of the colonial architecture in this country needs to be de-lionised. Discounting for the moment the geographical disadvantages of territory and climate, British nostalgia for the home country very often produced buildings and monuments which were impractical, awkward and at times completely out of sync with the times. The clash of Classical and Gothic architecture added to the confusion. We also come across imitation Swiss chalets and mock Tudor constructions that had very little to do with a country which for the most part is either hot, dry, rainy and in parts, even cold. Unlike China's decision to consciously underplay the Western (British colonial) presence, India did not obliterate these associations. The successors to the Raj continued to use the monuments the British built as public utilities such as government offices, universities, hospitals, railway stations, clubs and many others. Indeed many people in this country continue to celebrate and venerate these buildings.Others have no idea what to do with them. The SDO's bungalow in Vishnupur, where I was born, is now used as a godown and Warren Hastings' palatial garden house in Baraset another building with which I was familiar as a child, is in a state of decay and utter neglect. It may have to be pulled down. In my previous book Colonial Calcutta: Religious Architecture as a Mirror of Empire (Bloomsbury 2012), I made the point that the colonial ethic in the Americas where the British were themselves settlers and their attitudes and postures in India and elsewhere in South and South East Asia where the sole purpose was commerce and plunder, were totally divergent. Secondly, after the wars of the 1750s and 1760s when Calcutta was restyled as the political capital of Bengal and subsequently, following the Parliamentary Acts of 1773 and 1784, as the capital of British India, the white high steepled churches and monuments to the dead, rather than any of the native or other foreign religious shrines helped to connect Calcutta with the wider community of Empire. It was a question of how best sovereignty could be made visible to a conquered race. Western stylistic influences undoubtedly played a major role in this exercise. Most Colonial buildings were copied from pattern books and the so called Georgian/ Palladian buildings across the sub continent were designed and built by Army engineers. They fell a prey to the ravages of the tropical climate. The Indo Saracenic style of architecture, incorporated a mixture of Oriental motifs grafted onto more prosaic Western models, the intention being to ensure a kind of "continuity" with the previous rulers by selectively reading the cultural and architectural landscapes created by them. This trend appears to have gained momentum in the 19th century.

In fact, the Indo Saracenic movement established itself as a distinct, albeit separate, statement. I have never found Indo Saracenic buildings particularly inspiring because of their blatant and often overdone hybridity. Not all of the non conformist architecture of Chennai is either relevant or beautiful. So too, many of Bombay's (Mumbai's) heritage buildings like the Victoria Terminus, the Royal Bombay Yacht Club, the Prince of Wales Museum not to mention the Municipal Headquarters or the Office of the Commissioner of Police in the Apollo Bunder area, are examples of this kind of free and unbridled architectural treatment. Speaking of Mumbai, a city I lived in for over 25 years, Aldous Huxley once wrote that to him, Bombay was (architecturally) "one of the most apalling cities of either hemisphere" and that it had "the misfortune to develop during what was perhaps, the darkest period of all architectural history." Another traveller, Robert Byron, writing a few years later in the *Architectural Review* described it as an "architectural Sodom" and its buildings as "positively daemoniac." Yet another journal, the *Bombay Builder* (1860) was scathing in its criticism of the work by Wilkins and Stevens two names identified by locals as "distinguished" Indo Saracenic architects[1] I believe it was Mark Cousins, Director of History and Theory at the Architectural Association in London who, commenting on the "Ugly" in one of his lectures, made the point that phonies in the context of architecture were not necessarily a bad thing provided there was authenticity beyond simply "a homage that lies within an architectural sequel".[2] Another well known British art critic, Stephen Bayley echoes the same sentiments in a different context.[3] What I think both intended to convey was that a combination of undigested elements ceases to be beautiful unless viewed in the context of their time and circumstance. These and many other analytical aspects of the Indo Saracenic style have now come into focus and examined in depth by a host of post colonial historians. I have picked a few which I thought were relevant in the context of Irwin's work. While it is not possible to wish away history, there may be a case for moving away from unbridled acclaim for a movement which was not destined to endure for more than five decades. Even as a product of pre Independence India, I confess to a certain prejudice against the lack of objectivity by persons who benefitted materially from the Raj and those who blindly extolled its virtues. A craving for the foreign (British then, American now) unfortunately still persists. Very little is known of India's secular architecture because most of it, like the palace at Padmanabhapuram in Kerala was made out of timber and has not survived. The secular architecture of the Vijayanagar Empire at Hampi is better preserved but much of it, alas, is also in ruins. Unlike Europe there were no written architectural treatises or records which could be used to reconstruct regional styles. Indian indifference and apathy to treating antiquity as an academic discipline, no doubt also helped. In any case the Colonial government did not see much point in encouraging such effort. The Muslim conquest of India ended by generating a host of centrifrugal tendencies in the sub continent, mostly pro British and anti French, so that the desecration of several ancient monuments by the Colonial power in North and South India went virtually unnoticed even upheld. The subsequent imposition of a hybrid style of architecture with pronounced Islamic/ Byzantine motifs may have seemed weird and impractical at the time but had decisive undertones.

This book is divided into 10 chapters with accompanying illustrations as applicable. It examines Irwin's professional life in this country against the background of the political debate about a suitable pan Indian architectural style and some of the reasons why the Indo Saracenic movement failed to take off in the way its protagonists had hoped. Later personalities of the Indo Saracenic movement such as Emerson, Wittet, Begg and Swinton whose work was confined mainly to Western India, helped to put it on a firmer footing. However with the patronage of the Viceroy Lord Dufferin, Irwin seems to have had the freedom to experiment with his own ideas. He was also assisted by a few noteworthy associates. Chapter 1 deals with Architecture and the Colonial State. It examines the background of the Indo Saracenic style and some of the grammar necessary to appreciate the attitudes of the colonial state. Chapter 2, Eclecticism or Eccentricity discusses the Colonial discourse on a style of architecture suitable to Indian conditions, focussing on the British penchant for ornamentalism as a justification of sovereignty and Empire. The next chapter deals with Irwin's early life and his spectacular rise from a PWD Executive Engineer to Consulting Architect. Chapter 4 examines the building of the parish church in Panchmarhi, followed by (Chapter 5) the circumstances that led to his meeting with Dufferin and building the Viceregal Lodge in Simla (Shimla). This chapter contains excerpts from Lady Dufferin's memoirs with vivid descriptions of the interior of the building.The next two chapters cover Irwin's main projects in South India including various buildings in Madras (Chennai) and the Amba Vilas Palace in Mysore (Karnataka). The three concluding chapters examine some of the forces that operated to undermine the movement and why in the end it proved to be less popular than conceived or intended. I have added a chronological Appendix to trace Henry Irwin's professional life and work on the sub continent and another with illustrations about the architectural styles popular in Britain after 1550. A third Appendix identifies the Mughal ethos which was sought, unsuccessfully, to be copied Hopefully this will assist readers to identify some of the links which shaped the colonial architecture of British India. As far as possible, I have used the colonial names of the metropolitan cities referred to in this book with their current names in brackets, as applicable. Thereafter, I have reverted to their colonial identities.

My grateful thanks are due to the Publishers of this book, Partridge Publishing, a Penguin Random House Company, for their attentive and helpful support; to MARG Publications, Mumbai for identifying several articles on Victorian and Edwardian architecture in their previous issues, now unfortunately out of print; the Librarians of the National Library and Calcutta Club in Kolkata and the National Centre for the Performing Arts, Mumbai, not forgetting private collections in Chennai, for their help and many constructive suggestions; Ms Mabyn Pickering of Wrexham, UK, for sending me two rare volumes of Lady Dufferin's memoirs; Mr Hemanta Sengupta, who helped to illustrate the text with his eye catching pen and ink sketches and Amita, who spared valuable time for patiently wading through the text and footnotes, besides providing a few remarkably productive and innovative ideas. Amita was my best friend, mentor and worst critic for all of 58 years, before I lost her to a largely undiagnosed ailment recently. This book is dedicated to her memory. Finally, I am humbled by the wealth of post colonial scholarship led by stalwarts like Thomas Metcalf, Giles Tillotson, David Cannadine, Peter Scriver, Vikramaditya Prakash, Ashok Nangia and many others for their erudite and detailed work on the philosophy and mechanics behind the Indo Saracenic movement. But for their painstaking and committed research, I feel sure I would have found myself wallowing in uncertainties, forty miles out at sea without a paddle!

Pradip Kumar Das
Kolkata, 2014

Notes

1. Quoted in Gillian Tindall: City of Gold (London, Penguin 1982)
2. Mark Cousins: A series of articles on The Ugly in the AA files, 2012
3. Stephen Bayley: Ugly, The Aesthetics of Everything (Overlook Hardcover 2013)

CHAPTER 1

ARCHITECTURE AND
THE COLONIAL STATE

Indo Saracenic architecture–an architectural movement introduced by the British Government in India to legitimize their occupation and colonization of India was an attempt at "Orientalising" Western architectural forms. More importantly it was the centre of a debate to project British sovereignty over a conquered race. The style which essentially combined elements of Oriental "exoticism" like domes, vaulted roofs, kiosks, towers, minarets, scalloped or cusped arches, lattice work, harem windows and other features, with Victorian neo Gothic styles generated considerable controversy in its time. One of its early players was Henry Irwin, much of whose work and the legacy he left behind as a leading figure of Indo Saracenic architecture in South India, is the subject matter of this book. That his success had much to do with the patronage extended to him by the Viceroy of India, is relevant. Lord Dufferin, who occupied the position at the time, set aside considerations of seniority to propel his protégé first through a CIE onto a status, I suspect, much beyond Irwin's dreams. The Dufferin papers include a vast amount of India-related material and Irwin's elevation contained all the elements of an Irish fairy tale. The fact that both the Viceroy and Irwin were Irish may have been pure coincidence. In policy matters and on a personal level Dufferin was something of a moderate. He did not much care either for Anglo India, by which historians refer to the English in India, or about the small section of educated Indians whom he found precocious. His paternalism was directed more to the princely representatives of feudal India whose tastes and preferences he likened to his own.

It will be appreciated that in the context of Colonial India's building scenario in the mid 19th century, qualified, architects were a rare commodity. European "surveyors" or "master artificers" were less than professional architects. They had no formal architectural training. Although marginally superior to East India Company Army Engineers, they designed buildings and created drawings to suit a particular taste or fancy. This involved pattern books, grafts and even designing different parts of a building to suit individual preferences.They were leaders in the building process and worked hand in hand with masons, brick layers, and carpenters for the structure of the building, carvers for the exterior and joiners and plasterers for the interiors. Under this system, elaborate drawings were not required for the building because changes could be made throughout the process.

Around the time when Henry Irwin arrived in India there were a range of architectural styles prevailing in England, starting from the Regency and Italianate styles popular in the 1840s and 50s to the neo Renaissance and Gothic Revival, prevalent during the 1850s to 1880s. Thereafter, the Queen Anne style gained ground and the Edwardian, both of which witnessed the last sustained period of British architecture during the 19th century. All of these styles had certain common features, such as bay windows, dentils, columns, dormers, clapboard sidings, cornices, entablatures, gables, pediments, lintels, porticos, mansard roofs, transoms and turrets. This conglomeration of ideas led to architectural styles ranging from the comprehensible to the extravagant both in the home country and abroad. One is reminded of the Royal Pavilion at Brighton, a basically Georgian building compounded of Indian Gothic and Chinese elements. It was a piece of fanciful architecture which flourished throughout the greater part of the century besides giving self styled architects like Irwin a wide range of choices to experiment with, in his new assignment.

Individuals like Irwin had free access to these elements. Besides building commodities a number of designs were imported from England during the period. Irwin himself seems to have favoured the neo Renaissance style of his time, sometimes known as the Jacobethan (a combination of Elizabethan and Jacobean) architecture. The style was native to England and lent itself to further modifications to suit Indian conditions. The Railway Headquarters, the Town Hall and the Army barracks in Simla, all of which he designed, bear testimony to this style. One of Dufferin's first engagements in Simla was to inaugurate the Ripon Hospital, also designed by Irwin, in the Jacobethan style. It was made almost entirely of cedar (deodar) wood which is plentiful in Himachal and so impressed the new Viceroy that it earned Irwin the title of Superintendent of Works Imperial Circle. In fact one of Dufferin's first formal engagements in Simla was to inaugurate the new hospital. "It is a very pretty building . . . with accommodation for natives, Europeans and paying patients," wrote Lady Dufferin in her memoirs.[1] However, Irwin's main claim to fame was the design and execution of the Viceregal Lodge (now the Institute of Advanced studies) on Observatory Hill. Dufferin personally supervised the building of this mansion which contains several modifications suggested by the Viceroy.

Curzon (Viceroy of India from 1898-1905) did not seem to care too much about Irwin's work in Simla. He described the British summer resort as "Nothing more than a middle class suburb on a hill top." The Viceroy's Lodge struck the Curzons as odiously vulgar. "I keep trying not to be disappointed," confessed Lady Curzon, "A Minneapolis millionaire would revel in it."[2] Edwin Lutyens, too, was critical of Simla's hybrid architecture. Notwithstanding these deprecatory remarks about his work, Irwin left Simla in 1888 in a blaze of glory to take up his new elevated position in the Madras Presidency.

The term "Saracenic", is, of course, inappropriate. It is derived from a word used by the ancient Romans to refer to a people who lived in desert areas in and around the Roman province of Arabia who were distinct from the Arabs. It was also known as Indo Gothic, Mughal Gothic, Neo Gothic, Hindoo or Hindu Gothic and was criticised in the mother country as an architecture of folly. Basically it was an attempt by the colonial Administration to "Orientalise" typically Western tastes and forms in the hope that it would appeal to their Indian subjects. It was particularly prominent in Madras (now Chennai) and later spread to other parts of India. However Indo Saracenic buildings were much prized in the communities in which they were built. This could have been due to their innovative and "magical" appearance or, by comparison to native secular architecture, a style which seemed to incorporate a grand fusion of European and Indian elements.The appeal rested on the twin functions of association and sensual effect. Indo Saracenic architecture, like sculpture, struck popular imagination by the size of its buildings, mass, space, colour and texture. These buildings were confined to public spaces like government offices, municipalities, law courts, colleges, museums and art galleries and therefore enjoyed greater visibility. Some reaped the benefits of princely patronage and some others were grafted onto buildings in the territories under British occupation as representing their (the Imperial) concept of Indian heritage architecture.

Colonial India accepted this latter explanation because by and large, a subject population had little say in the way public buildings of the Raj were designed. A few Indians, like D.R. Bhandarkar and others, were endowed with a sense of history. Even a person of his calibre could write about the excavations in Mohenjo Daro as "the ruins of a town not more than 200 years old" because "the bricks here found are of the modern type and there is a total lack of carved terracotta amidst the whole ruins."[3] There were no written or reliable architectural treatises from the past, and communal divisions were permitted to disrupt, if not to destroy the architectural evidence of centuries. Because of the difficulty in deciphering scripts nobody cared to document or to examine the ethos and character of secular buildings in these ancient cities not to speak of power centres like Pataliputra or Kanauj under former Indian dynasties like the Mauryas and Guptas. The British made serious attempts to do so, but eventually succeeded in persuading their native subjects to accept the colonial interpretation and perception of our legacies with ill concealed admiration. Most Indians, even today, eulogise Indo Saracenic buildings as "magnificent" pieces of architecture, although the overall effect of the style was that of unfamiliar and often obsessive ornamentation. The earlier "architects" of the movement were glorified engineers without formal training. They followed the political diktat of the times and the movement came to occupy a significant chapter in the evolution of Indian architecture. However, its passage was fleeting. Its aesthetics and relevance have been questioned and made the subject of separate post colonial study. Significantly, Indo Saracenic architecture never found its way into residential complexes or to the homes of ordinary people.

Buildings and monuments can be read in many ways. Architecture–the art of building–has a language of its own and reading buildings is just like reading in any other language. Basically three key aspects make up the grammar of this language: First: Period based styles Second: different building types and Third, structural materials. All of these greatly influence the way a building looks.

Within this "grammatical" structure there is an architectural vocabulary of individual building parts such as columns, fireplaces, roofs, stairs, windows and doors. Decorative ornamentation, domes, spires and steeples are also important elements of this vocabulary.

The function of a building can influence its appearance and many types of buildings have distinctive features that make them easy to recognise. Examples are a church tower, a temple gateway or a mosque dome. Do they stand witness to the rapacity and self delusion of empire? Are they monuments to a world of lost glory and forgotten convictions? Do they reveal battles won by invidual cultures and styles? Or do they simply represent an architectural style made absurdly incongruous in relocation?

Many more questions come to mind. For example:

(i) How far did racial theory and political/religious agendas guide British architects? Were such ideas resisted when applied? In the case of Indo Saracenic architecture, the subject matter of the present book, a section of architectural historians agree that the experiment was largely a failure because it was an imposition from the top with foreign concepts working through the medium of traditional craftspersons merely mimicking prescribed forms.

(ii) Did imported building types organise space in such a way that imperial power was produced?

(iii) Is such power reproducible simply by replicating these building types?

(iv) Apart from the well known evolution of the "bungalow" were there other indigenous spatial structures adopted to colonial modern uses?

(v) How did the characteristic spatial structures of the different regional and historical building traditions of India respond to and/or resist the changing spatial practices and prerogatives of colonial times?

(vi) How in post colonial times have such structures been revalued and reinstated into the colonisers' buildings by spatial/structural transformation?

The many loyal ovations to the Raj obscure or blur many of these questions. The facts are that despite all their attempts to "enshrine their sovereignty in stone, teak marble and bronze"[4] and unlike the domestic and public architecture in many South East Asian countries, the British failed to develop a living pan Indian style of architecture for India. The priorities of the Colonial state were not to discover and nurture the historical roots of Indian building traditions but to use them more as interesting cultural curiosities which could be linked to current (18th century) paintings of the "exotic" in Britain, if not also as a viable proposition for commercial profitability. Even Fergusson's documentations of old Indian buildings, considered as the first comprehensively written account of Indian architecture and as primary source material among colonial scholars of Indian art and architecture, were in many ways controversial and divisive. In the ultimate analysis Fergusson was convinced of the "unworthiness" of Indian architecture and regarded all that was beautiful or significant in that area was a result of Greek or Roman influences. The late 19th and early 20th centuries saw a swing away from Fergusson's theories, focussing on Indian crafts. It was propagated by the British artistic intelligentsia led by William Morris and others. However these representations were defeated in the face of political considerations.

The average run of urban British Indian architecture, prompted both by missionary zeal as much as the British penchant to "improve" Indian lifestyles, such as law courts, government offices, insurance companies, trading houses schools, colleges, libraries clubs, gymkhanas all came into their own from around the middle of the 19th century. "Govern them and lift them up for ever" was the inscription proposed by Lutyens for the Viceroy's House in New Delhi, a 285 room palace larger than Versailles, where much to Churchill's disgust, a loin cloth clad Gandhi met the Representative of the King Emperor in 1931.[5] Other civic structures included railway and police stations, jails and cantonments They were created by professional institutionalised agencies geared to meet the needs of the Colonial government and did not impact India's rural majority.

Notes

1. Lady Harriet Dufferin: Our Viceregal Life in India (London, John Murray, 1889)
2. Niall Fergusson: Empire (Allen Lane 2003 & Penguin 2004)
3. John Keay: A History of India, (Harper Perennial 2004)
4. Peter Scriver & Vikramaditya Prakash: Colonial Moderniies (Routledge 2007)
5. Niall Fergusson: Empire (Allen Lane 2003 & Penguin 2004)

CHAPTER 2

ECLECTICISM OR ECCENTRICITY

The Indo Saracenic movement elicited mixed responses from traditionalists and modernists alike. Starting with British interests in the Middle East and Egypt at a time when Orientalism was fashionable, the Indo Saracenic style was basically imititative of the traditional architectural styles of the Middle East and India, without much understanding of the structural values that gave this country its distinctive character–much like popular Western interpretations of Yoga or Hindustani classical music, which liken them to aerobic exercises on the one hand and to improvisations in modern jazz on the other. The idea of course was to represent to the 300 odd Indian princes left after the collapse of the Mughal empire that this was a form of architecture which represented their own heritage, albeit in a Westernised form. The wave lasted until the Viceroyalty of Lord Curzon (1898-1905) when the Government decided that Imperialism could only be mirrored in a European style.

Indeed, the architectural history of Colonial India emanates from the debate on whether the fusion of Western and Oriental design were more desirable for projecting the image of the British Empire than by examples of buildings and monuments which were passed off as "classical" or "neo classical" or "revivalist" without incorporating the basic elements of the originals. Those who built these monuments obviously did so taking advantage, as historian Giles Tillotson observes[1], of local ignorance of the grammar of the European classical language. The nineteenth century greatly influenced many of us–particularly those in the generation preceding mine–because they have so much to tell us of the history of colonialism and cultural exchange.

When the East India Company and later the British Government, became involved in establishing and projecting their sovereignty on the subcontinent, it was also a period of several historic and political cross currents which left their imprint on the colonial culture of British India. As one critic points out, the decline of the Mughal empire and its successor states created shock waves in the intellectual world of London and elsewhere. There was plunder and military conquest of course but these were coupled with attempts to develop a style of imperialism which would, on the one hand, identify with their own, and to a lesser extent, the aspirations of their subjects, by harking back to the ancient Mughal constitution to support a theory of continuity.

Early Company buildings were simple and functional. However, with the spread of colonialism, East India Company officers who were basically traders and business persons, needed to connect with the local rulers as part of conscious policy. Therefore, they looked for an architectural style which would have local appeal and at the same time, reflect the rulers' concern over expressions of power. Unfortunately they underestimated the wide variety of architectural styles across the country.

Most British colonial buildings in India sported arcades and deep verandahs besides louvred doors and windows, to deal with the needs of the tropical climate. However, because they were designed from pattern books by Army engineers even as late as the mid 19th century, they did not conform to the originals and were deficient in structural elements. Following the establishment of the Public Works Department, many of these buildings were commissioned and regulated according to set rules and procedures. This placed restrictions on creative work. There were other issues. A group of Native Revivalists headed by persons like E.B.Havell, James Fergusson and Percy Brown thought that civic architecture should represent the people, something with a connection to the land and the past, which in later Victorian times was mirrored by William Morris' Arts and Craft's view–of returning to an architecture using craftsmanship and traditional methods. This was opposed by another section of the Government which was emphatic in the belief that like the Romans who carried their architecture with them, British Imperialism must also reflect the ideology of empire through their buildings as physical manifestations of colonial authority. The Industrial Revolution offered construction simplification by the widespread use of imported iron and other raw materials but tended to restrict architectural ingenuity. There was also considerable bureaucratic manipulation. Sharada Dwivedi and Rahul Mehrotra in their book, *The Cities Within* refer for example, to James Ransome, Consulting Architect to the Governmnent of India who was told to make Calcutta classical, Bombay Gothic and Madras Saracenic. There were many other issues. Bombay's stone carvers were able to work with better grade stone than others, public and residential buildings in Calcutta and Madras were by and large, made of sun dried bricks coated with stucco. The result was that over time, many of these buildings eventually fell into disrepair. British Engineers on colonial service also adversely influenced the training of Indian technicians. The trend continued until Indian Independence.

The English East India Company had been trading in the sub continent since the 17th century. It was not until the mid 19th century that the British crown had formally proclaimed its Raj or imperial authority over India and thereby fully assumed the obligations of a colonial government. The typical buildings of the company era with their fortifications gave way to more and more elegant architectural design. By the late 19th century the public buildings of the Raj had come to exhibit a conspicuously flamboyant romanticism. This was characterised by a mixture of decorative features and details derived from the more spectacular architecture of India's pre Colonial past–the palaces of the Rajput princes in particular–but not excluding the inspiration of other exotic architectures of the Orientalist imagination such as China. The so called Indo Saracenic style found its earliest patrons among the princely Indian rulers of the nominally independent states within the enveloping geographical matrix of British India, but by 1870 it was becoming the preferred style for the public architecture for British India as well.

Following the events of 1857 and the proclamation of Queen Victoria as "Empress of India" an outward change in the pattern of governance of the country became palpable. One of these was the Imperial desire to identify themselves as Trustees of India's ancient heritage rather than as rapacious alien rulers. The Indo Saracenic style came to represent a conscious move in this direction. However there were other considerations. One of these was the British appetite for grand architecture to rival anything the Mughal administration had done before and to establish themselves as natural successors to the previous rulers. "We are trustees for India's intellectual and material possessions" annouced E.B. Havell at a meeting of the East India Association in the 1900s. "We have Imperial pledges to fulfill. India, the real India needs a renaissance of her own art."[2] He was supported among others by James Fergusson and F.S. Growse.

In an interesting essay entitled "Ornamentalism," another British historian, David Cannadine, has argued that one of the aspects of British Imperialism in India was the rulers' obsession with ostentation and ornamentalism.[3] According to Cannadine, this went beyond the "stereotypical view of racial superiority and collective antagonism" and in turn, translated into the "plume and plummage" to replicate and magnify the social order of the home country. It also enabled members of the Colonial government to share the same platform with groups of the Indian elite–its princes, sultans and nawabs. For the latter, who notwithstanding their Westernisation were keen to project their "Indian" identity, the new style of building public spaces and palaces was something of a novelty and an excuse to adopt a Western architectural model which seemed to blend with their own. The obsession with Orientalism went as far as to influence Queen Victoria herself to add a new wing to her official residence (Osborne House) in England which had a marked resemblance to the interiors of a Mughal palace. To what extent this "obsession with ostentation and ornamentalism" was a posture of social equality with the Indian elite is difficult to assess. Racial considerations, like the time when the future King Edward VII insisted on the Hawaiin King Kalalaua's presence at a royal gathering but with a twist, reflect attitudes that echo throughout the corridors of the British empire. Edward is supposed to have insisted that the man was "Either a king or a common garden nigger".It is for consideration if the King of

England could have described any of his relatives or European royalty in these terms.

The baffling variety of shapes and designs in the heartland of Mughal India not to speak of the artistic traditions elsewhere on the subcontinent specially in Rajasthan, Madhya Pradesh, Tamil Nadu and elsewhere in the Deccan were obstacles in the way of defining a truly representative Indian architectural style. Not surprisingly, therefore, a hybrid style of building emerged which even today many people find culturally disturbing.

Contemporary British opinion on the subject was also divided. Some rather facetious remarks by Edwin Lutyens, the architect of Imperial New Delhi, in his early days are relevant. If a "Hindu" structure were required," he wrote, "set square stones and build childwise, but before you erect, carve every stone differently and independently, with lace patterns and terrifying shapes. On top over trabeated pendentives, set an onion." If the choice were Mughal, he continued, built a vasty mass of rough concrete, elephantwise on a very simple rectangular-cum-octagonal plan, dome in anyhow, cutting off square. Overlay with a veneer of stone patterns, like laying a vertical tile floor and get Italians to help you . . . Then on top of the mass put three turnips in concrete and overlay with stone or marble as before. Be very careful not to bond anything in, and don't care a damn if it all comes to pieces." While these observations display the overt arrogance of the man, not to speak of ignorance, his remarks on British

Indo Saracenic were more specific. In describing the style as the Raj's own "particular form of vulgarity" he was equally dismissive of the capabilities of some of his contemporaries.[3] The issue was not so much about the preservation of an ancient heritage but about a style of architecture which, as Thomas Metcalf observes, would project British sovereignty over the subcontinent.[4] It is significant that buildings in the Indo Saracenic style had already begun to make their appearance before Swinton Jacob, an architect in the employ of the Maharaja of Jaipur, had compiled his collection of over six hundred drawings taken from North Indian buildings some as early as the 12th century, of copings, plinths, arches, brackets and so on, presumably with the intention of using them as elements of fusion in the buildings designed by him. Besides Jacob other architects/engineers included names like Robert Chisholm, Charles Mant, Henry Irwin, William Emerson, George Wittet and Frederick Stevens. However 1890 represents the formal birth of the Indo Saracenic movement and Jacob's Portfolio, as the collection was called, gave the Colonial rulers the confidence they needed to declare themselves in control of India's architectural heritage and to present their work as authentic representations of a British Indian style. However, in more than one instance, the results were outlandish. At the Muir College at Allahabad, Tillotson came across a large hall which exuded a "vague air of Venetian Gothic", a dome which was "Mughal in outline but Persian in decoration" and a minaret "which appeared to have been transposed from Mamluk in Egypt."[5]

The process of "orientalising" an alien architectural form created a number of problems and was, perhaps, flawed from its inception. To start with, the designs were imposed from the top, without any adherence to the stylistic canons prevalent in a particular period. They did not embody the insights and thoughts which went into building the originals. Consequently these later Victorian adaptations embodying Oriental grafts onto a conventional European architectural framework were unlikely to reflect the ethos and aesthetics which guided earlier rulers.

Secondly, despite protests by Havell and many others, Indian participation in building these monuments was limited to crafting and executing the designs created by a group of foreigners. They were not consulted about the redefinition process, much less given the authority to make any major contributions at the concept, design or drawing board stages.

Thirdly, the much touted "British" architecture projected by that country and exported to the colonies as its very own, was itself a mixture of styles–from the beauxarts classicism of Europe with its straight lines, columns and triangular pediments to Jacobethan with its flattened Tudor arches, lighter stone trims, carved brickwork gabled roofs, porticoes and balustrades down to the movement known as Revival Gothic a style of architecture deeply intertwined with the philosophic movements associated with the growth of non conformism in the home country. These styles and building techniques were not always applicable to India even if they were appropriate to the white settler colonies of say New Zealand Australia or Canada. Besides lacking in architectural purity it would require a person with a lot of courage to blend them into an aesthetic Eastern form.

The real issue was, of course, political. The Indo Saracenic movement was caught up in the controversy created by the Colonial government about the manner in which it wanted to assert and project its Imperialist image. Hardinge, (Viceroy of India from 1910-1916) and other partisans of the movement including Baker, were in favour of "orientalising" British architecture in India. They believed that times were changing and that the Government of India should now be seen as a joint British Indian enterprise, even as Emerson, himself a protagonist of the Indo Saracenic style, suggested that it was "impossible for the architecture of the West to be suitable to the natives of the East." Curzon (1898-1905) was firmly opposed to the idea. He argued the case that "a non Indian, Western and foreign system" of government "could not be satisfied by Indian or Asiatic architectural forms."[6] He was of course guided by Colonial Calcutta's version of Palladian architecture, the city that had served as the Capital of British India for over 200 years.

Lutyens described Jacob as someone who was a gentleman but not an architect. However it is significant that by the time the capital of British India moved from Calcutta to Delhi, and Lutyens had been assigned to design the Imperial capital, he went ahead with a plan that would overcome all objections. By this time Lutyens had matured sufficiently to know that the indigenous architecture of the subcontinent was without parallel in many aspects and that to ignore it would be to display a conspicuous lack of knowledge of its treasures and antiquity. He therefore initiated a strategy that was far superior in concept to anything the Indo Saracenics had produced–a style which went beyond the superficialities of graft and unassimilated forms. It was imaginative, original and above all, aesthetically pleasing. It drew on symbolic abstractions and ideas rather than direct copies, to create an overall impression of elegance and grandeur to rival Shahjehan's capital if not also Imperial Rome. Although technically a blend of Edwardian elegance with all that was picturesque in Indian architecture, the stunning fusion of ideas drawn from Hindu, Islamic, Buddhist and European classical sources was enough to leave contemporaries standing. It also seemed to satisfy Imperial objectives. Indeed, following the completion of his assignment, Lutyens was described by his own colleagues as one of the greatest architects of Empire.

It is equally significant that but for a few rare examples, the Indo Saracenic style hardly touched Christian religious architecture in Colonial India. While Gothic ornamentation with its pointed arches and vaulted roofs could conceivably lend itself to orientalisation, the English architect A.W.N. Pugin equated Gothic architecture with "Christian" architecture. He stressed its rationality and penchant for detail, very different from the "heathen" implications of onion shaped domes, minarets and indeed, even of neo classical or Graeco Roman monuments. Also, as colonial records indicate, it was possible to build two evangelist churches for the price of one in the Baroque or Palladian styles! Finally Gothic had the endorsements of all the known authorities in England, the Church Commissioners, the Camden Society and the Ecclesiologist. That this point was not lost on the Anglo Indian designers is evident from the fact that like his predecessors and contemporaries, Henry Irwin himself, avoided the unconventional when designing the Christian church in Panchmarhi which still bears his name.

The city of Madras best reflects examples of Irwin's work, a style that locals find fascinating. Others, eager to conserve these monuments, as an integral part of India's heritage are defensive about the aesthetics. These quaint buildings with their mixed bag of rectangular towers pointed arches and clearly unassimilated adornments, some vaguely Mughal others distinctly Moorish, have now become the subject of critical enquiry and appraisal in the growing field of architectural history and theory. Some, sadly have been left to languish in the face of official/ bureaucratic neglect.

Notes

1. G.H.R. Tillotson: The Tradition of Indian Architecture, Continuity and Change since 1850 (New Haven:Yale University Press)
2. T. Metcalf: An Imperial Vision: Indian Architecture and Britain's Raj (University of California Press, Berkeley and Los Angeles)

3. Ibid

4. Ibid.

5. G.H.R. Tillotson: Orientalising the Raj (Marg, Vol 46 no1 1986)

6. T. Metcalf: Op. Cit

CHAPTER 3

AN IRISH ENGINEER IN SEARCH OF A STYLE

Henry Irwin was born on 21st January 1841 to an Irish Catholic family in Tarbett, County Kerry, Southern Ireland. He and his father shared a common Christian name. The senior Irwin was Archdeacon of Killukin, County Roscommon, Southern Ireland. Henry Irwin Jr. began his professional career in 1864 in the Admiralty of the United Kingdom as a Surveyor of Coastguard Buildings. Before then he qualified as a Member of the Institute of Civil Engineers in the UK and was subsequently posted, in 1866, to the Department of Public Works in Ceylon (Sri Lanka). However he does not appear to have acquired a degree or a diploma in architecture. After a spell of two years, in 1868, he was transferred to India in the same Department. Irwin's initiation to the colonial brand of architecture in this country was the design of a church in Panchmarhi when he was Executive Engineer in Nagpur (1872). The building was designed and built in accordance with the guidelines laid out for ecclesiastical buildings in the UK in the 19th century which abhorred not only onion domes and pointed arches but even the "heathen" implications of the neo classical or Graeco Roman monuments. It was a movement known as the Gothic Revival and associated with a reawakening of High Church or Anglo Catholic self belief as a reaction to the destruction of Christian values by non conformists and industrialisation. Later, following various assignments in the Department of Public Works, Irwin moved to Simla (Shimla) in 1881. Four years later, in 1884, he was to meet the then Viceroy of India, Lord Dufferin, a meeting which would result in many honours being heaped upon him, including his appointment as Consulting Architect to the Madras Government in 1888.

Irwin's predecessor in Madras was Robert Fellowes Chisholm, considered to be one of the pioneers of the Indo Saracenic movement. Chisholm's style was totally different from Irwin's, although, like Irwin, not much is known about his early education. Henry Irwin was less driven. He continued the Indo Saracenic style of building guided in the main by the more utilitarian parameters set by the PWD. Meanwhile, as Peter Scriver observes, westernised Indian tastes endorsed the pseudo Indic approach to the design of modern public buildings.[1] These sentiments were echoed by some of the princely states who were quick to seize the advantages of the

British presence in return for unquestioning loyalty. They too were good meat for the Indo Saracenics. To quote from a poem composed by one such individual:

"Glorious and mighty is England's rule in India
Blessed are the people that have a Ruler so benevolent
Constant has been thy aim to promote Thy subjects' welfare
Loving and protecting them like a kind hearted father:
Oh! Where shall we get a noble ruler like Thee![1]

With attitudes like these, which almost mirror the strains of our own National Anthem, it is not surprising that the Indo Saracenic movement struck deep roots in India, gained momentum and flourished beyond the Madras and Bombay Presidencies in many provincial capitals and some princely states. It was the kind of architecture which immediately announced to the natives the "benevolent" presence of their English masters and gave them a means–or so the English believed–of identifying with foreign rule. It is significant in this connection that the English were less concerned with India's Hindu or Buddhist past, and that even in Madras they completely bypassed the great architectural traditions of the Pallavas and Cholas, in favour of a pseudo Islamic identity. Indeed the pointed arch and dome came to be regarded as the quintessential elements of this synthesis. Lord Napier, (Governor of Madras from 1866-1872 and Acting Viceroy from February to May 1872), believed that this architecture had Roman origins but as Thomas Metcalf notes the main objective of the exercise was to ape the power and majesty of the Mughal Empire, which the British now wished to claim as their own.[2]

It is equally surprising that the movement to "Islamise" public monuments in Madras was accepted without question by master builders like Thattikonda Namberumal Chetty, considered by many to have been Irwin's chief associate. Chetty acquired as many as 99 properties in his lifetime, including a locality named after him (Chetpet) in Madras city.[3] Obviously for Chetty as with his contemporaries the aura of British resources and presence overcame patriotic pride or pious Hindu intentions.

Comparisons are sometime drawn between Henry Irwin and Frederick Chisholm. Neither were trained architects but of the two, Chisholm was more gifted and had an independent vision. Chisholm came to Madras after winning a competition for the design of the Senate House and the Presidency College. Subsequently he also assumed the responsibility for running the Madras School of Art. The fact that he quickly fell in line with the fashion and politically correct mood of the time, disguises to an extent, his commitment to the concept that architecture and craftsmanship were very closely linked. His design of the Napier Museum in Trivandrum, drawing upon the use of wood in what he called the "native style" of the Malabar Coast, was based on the architecture of the region, in particular the old Travancore capital of Padmanabhapuram. It was very different fom the public buildings in Madras and proved his personal belief that an imported architecture to be accepted, must adapt itself to the climate and to the "requirements of the people." He decried the "thoughtless adoption" of the Gothic or any other European style to Indian architecture and advocated the promotion of architectural principles to influence building styles. Chisholm's proposals were of course defeated. In his address to the Royal Institute of British architects in 1873, Chisholm cited the architecture of the Padmanabhapuram palace in Travancore with its "stacked roofs of timber and tile construction" as his chief inspiration. Chisholm felt that both elements, not excluding dormers and railed brackets under the roof eaves to facilitate ventilation, were essential to buildings in India.

Chisholm was able to translate many of these ideas in designing and executing the Napier Museum in Travancore which bore the name of the acting Viceroy of India, at the time, Lord Napier. However, while Napier was more of a believer in the arts and crafts movement and less in the condition of architecture in both India and England, he did not agree that Chisholm's concept was suitable for a pan Indian colonial architecture beyond specific communities. Napier favoured the Indo Saracenic style because of its (mistakenly) assumed "Roman" origins and because of its suitability for "all the diversified requirements of modern social life." He cited Chisholm's Revenue Board Office and the Post and Telegraph buildings in Madras–not the Napier Museum– as seminal examples of his idea. Ironically, it was the Napier Museum that survived while the Post and Telegraph building like many others, fell a victim to ad hoc additions and, in time, its steep pitched roofs were also lost from its central towers.

From the outset, and throughout his tenure as Consulting Architect to the Government of Madras, Chisholm was involved with the Madras School of Arts and was temporarily placed in charge of that institution. He also proposed that the University of Madras should establish a Chair in architecture with the specific intention of training the local community who would build for India in the future and by whom the British colonisers would ultimately be judged. Unfortunately the idea did not then materialise and Chisholm's concept of the architect/craftsman relationship was also lost. The nature of the displays and the extent to which the Napier Museum met its targetted segment of visitors was the subject of a separate study, as were the architectural interventions that occurred in the aftermath of the Survey of Museums between 1928 and 1937.

Henry Irwin obviously lacked Chisholm's initiative or commitment. The buildings he designed were mostly mundane and utilitarian in line with PWD thinking. Those, like the Connemara Library and the Madras Victoria Memorial were faithful copies, dictated by political exigencies. They were not great works of art and both invited criticism because of their incongruity and lack of connectivity to the history of South India. As a disdainful professional observer who travelled to India around this time commented: "No Englisman is a settler in India. We do not transport ourselves, our houses and modes of life to that country. We only go there for a term of years, and consequently, looking at the whole thing as temporary, we put up with that which in a real colony would soon be superseded." The same observer goes on to say that the buildings that did get erected were "motley modern (with) no pretensions to architectural character."[4] Irwin's earlier creations, like the Church at Panchmarhi or the Viceregal Lodge at Simla were mediocre copies of British designs popular in the mother country at the time. Their alienation from the Indian environment was even more profound.

It is of course well known that architects and engineers approach projects from different perspectives. While an architect is concerned chiefly with creativity and design, engineers are more concerned with the mathematical aspects of a project, like its scientific base, budget and material costs. In either case there has to be a liason between the environment, design teams and the client. The observations made by the observer in the previous paragraph seem to indicate that like most British colonial institutions, Indo Saracenic architecture even in its later years, was an imposition from the top with no connections at all to local taste or sensitivity and only a superficial and fantasised resemblance to Indian cultural traditions and heritage. It is also doubtful if any of the engineer-architects exported to this country in the 19th century had the skills or the qualifications necessary to translate their own fanciful visions into quantifiable elements.

Between 1888 and 1896 Irwin designed and built several monuments in Madras some of which were completed after his death. In 1896 he retired to Mount Abu in Rajasthan. In 1897 he was invited by the ruler of Mysore the Queen Regent, Rani Vannivilasa, to design and rebuild the older royal palace destroyed by fire the previous year. It was the climax of a career which, among other things, established the questionable credentials of a foreign engineer in preference to indigenous crafts persons. Five years later, in 1922, Irwin moved to Loch End in Ootacamund, where he died on 5th August the same year.

Notes

1. Niall Ferguson: Empire London, (Allen Lane 2003 and Penguin 2004)
2. Thomas Metcalf: An Imperial Vision: Berkeley, (University of California Press 1989)
3. V. Sriram: The Architect of the Connemara Library and More (The Journalistic History of Madras, 2012)
4. Paul Walker quoted in Peter Scriver and Vikramaditya Prakash ed: Colonial Modernities (Routledge 2007)

PANCHMARHI: PARISH CHURCH AND TOWER

CHAPTER 4

PANCHMARHI: A CHURCH IN THE MOUNTAINS

In 1872, Henry Irwin was posted to Nagpur and the Central Provinces (Madhya Pradesh) as Executive Engineer in the PWD. Before then he married Henrietta Helen in 1871. Both husband and wife were devout Catholics. Church records indicate that in the nine years between 1872 and 1881 most of their children including two sons and seven daughters were born either in Nagpur or in Panchmarhi, a small hill resort—currently about a six hour drive away from Nagpur—which the family frequented. Panchmarhi had been "discovered" less than 20 years ago by a Captain Forsythe of the Bengal Lancers in 1857. It was, as Dane Kennedy writes, a quintessential British home away from home.[1] Panchmarhi was part of the Satpura range of hills with undulating valleys, tranquil forests and deep pools fed by streams that ran across the lava hills. In due course the British developed it as a military sanatorium and hot weather resort. In the 1870s it was still relatively undeveloped.

Like many other hill stations of the time, Panchmarhi's salubrious climate appealed to a section of the British community settled in the Central Provinces (now Madhya Pradesh) The report by John Sullivan, Collector of Coimbatore had already persuaded the British Government that health and leisure were important to their expatriate staff serving away from the coast in the landlocked areas of the country. Another survey revealed that mortality rates of British soldiers were lower for those living in the hills as opposed to those serving on the plains. It also became a summer resort for army personnel and their families escaping from the heat of the plains. The economy of Panchmarhi depended to a large extent on the presence of the army but there were also a number of private houses, most with gabled roofs, built in the colonial style. The Government of the Central Provinces (Madhya Pradesh) also used it as its official summer retreat, to which even today, Panchmarhi's Raj Bhavan stands testimony.

Panchmarhi was not socially or politically at the level of Simla or Darjeeling or Ootacamund but its layout and planning like the 80 odd hill stations built during this period, were modelled on an English village. Its central point was the Anglican or Catholic Church with its "Victorian Gothic solidity". A central avenue emanated from there with Government buildings like the Post and Telegraph Office, the

Magistrate's or SDO's office located along this thoroughfare including banks and shops. At various points along the way were winding lanes leading to private cottages across the undulating topography of the station. In Panchmarhi, some of these led to secluded reserves waterfalls and pools which continue to attract visitors—many with old British associations—such as Daisy Pool, Irene Pool, Duchess Falls, Piccadilly Circus, Bee Falls, Lansdowne Point and Fancy Pool.

The old cemetery in Panchmarhi shows a total of 237 burials (mainly British army personnel) over the period 1871-1941. The Burial Register, a copy of the original held by the SDO, Military Engineering Services, Panchmarhi, is currently held by the Anunciation Church, and while the plots categorised by the religious denominations shown in the register are not clearly defined in the cemetery, there is no obvious demarcation between Roman Catholic, Church of England or Non Conformist. The cemetery is small and in fair condition, although lately it has been a victim of neglect.[2]

The son of a British Warrant officer in the Army Education Corps, Walter Reeve, now settled in Australia, wrote about his "fascination and connection with Panchmarhi" in the 30's of the last century. The family stayed in Panchmarhi until mid 1941 and then again after a break in Ceylon (Sri Lanka) for a year from 1942 until 1943. After the Hindu Muslim hostilities of 1946 the family again returned to Panchmarhi but by then, most of the British families had left and Panchmarhi had become a "ghost town." They stayed at Mrs Booker's Hotel and finally left for Nowshera in 1947. Returning to India in 2003, he feared that Panchmarhi would have changed beyond recognition but was more than relieved to find it had not. "The house where we lived was still there, so was Mrs Booker's Hotel, albeit renamed, and so were the Golf course, the churches and my school. Eager to obtain pictures of everything that was familiar to me, I soon came across a tight security regime which prevented me from entering many areas except under escort."[3] In the course of his visit the writer met up with an old Indian colleague in the Army who was also staying at Mrs Booker's Hotel in 1946 and recalled a quarrel they had over "a trivial matter" that ended with him kicking the Indian officer's "sola topee" to pulp. He also recalled a visit to the British cemetery to find the grave of a little girl who he knew as a youngster and who died of malaria at the age of four.[4]

Irwin's contribution to the architecture of Panchmarhi was the town's 'Christ Church.' It is described by Vikram Bhatt from church records as "a small but beautifully crafted edifice. Its red and gold sandstone (native to the region) and a stunning set of stained glass windows give a unique glow to the interior."[5] In a Guide to Panchmarhi brought out by the C.P.Government Press Nagpur the church is described as a monument with a "fascinating architecture; its 'sanctum sanctorum' has a hemispherical dome on top with its ribs ending with faces of angels. The stained glass panes adorning the rear and walls of the altar, imported from Europe present a gorgeous view as the sun's rays pass through them." These descriptions are unfortunately overrated.

The best that can be said about the church was that it was a cross cultural copy of various European elements, spectacular in the semi rural environs of Panchmarhi but otherwise only an experiment which skirted "the inherently conservative if not reactionary colonial technocracy" of the Public Works Department. The PWD was the technical arm of the colonial Government staffed in the main by army engineers and specialised in a range of utilitarian buildings noted for their "strikingly chaste" and "parsimonius" simplicity. Typical of the criticisms of the unimaginative environment in which that Department operated is the following quote from Major J.G. Medley's *Anglo Indian Architecture* quoted by Peter Scriver which describes a typical PWD church of the period ". . . barn-like . . . differing only from a barrack in the presence of a square tower and classical (?) portico"[6] Medley was the Principal of the Thomason College of Engineering in Roorkee, Uttar Pradesh, set up to train Indian assistant engineers and subordinate staff for the PWD. It was the first civil engineering college to be set up not only in India but also in the rest of the British Empire. The description, albeit derisive and a little harsh, does not do justice to Irwin's creation although it does, to an extent, explain his own and the limitations under which he had to work.

James Betley, a freelance architectural historian describes, additionally, how comprehensive catalogues on church furnishings made their way in to the colonies. Sculptures, designs, and carvings were things one could easily pick out of the catalogue or the architect working on the church could design the fittings. These included altar frontals, candles, all the furniture and fittings, the lectern and so on. On occasion whole prefabricated structures were shipped out.[7] There can be little doubt that Irwin took full advantage of these facilities. In India, and especially in remote Panchmarhi, labour was cheap and anything "foreign" was much prized because the locals knew no better.

As a concession to the theological and philosophic movement known as Revival Gothic which England was witnessing at this time, the church incorporates a few of its essential features. The movement was based on a reawakening of High Church or Anglo Catholic self belief as a reaction to the destruction of Christian values by non-conformists and industrialisation. The English architect, A.W.N. Pugin equated Gothic architecture with "Christian" architecture. He stressed its rationality and penchant for detail. Perpendicular Gothic, the style largely exported to the colonies had strong vertical lines in window tracery and wall panellings, elaborately designed vaults and ceilings, with decorated and pinnacled towers. It possessed none of the "heathen" implications inherent in neo classical or Graeco Roman monuments and more importantly had the endorsement of all the known authorities in England, the Church Commissioners, the Camden Society and the Ecclesiologist. With its ornamentation, its pointed arches and vaulted roofs, Revival Gothic also lent itself to Orientalisation. Indeed, the style made concessions to the heat, rain and blazing light by the use of such devices as fixed wooden screens, porticoes and verandahs, shutters, hoods, lattice work and blinds while at the same time admitting cross currents of breeze, and to make maximum use of shade and shadows. Domes, kiosks and "harem windows" were all freely incorporated.

Symbolic of this English movement, was the quintessential Gothic Revival Porch the mandatory pitched roofs and gables, the tall stained glass lancet windows behind the altar serving a dual purpose–they had to be open to the roof and large enough to admit light and a bar tracery "rose" window, another standard feature of Revival Gothic. The square tower with its steeple was a significant style for churches in the nineteenth century and became associated with attempts to revive the perceived religious fervour of the Middle Ages. As for the dome, the idea was clearly borrowed from early Christian and Byzantine architecture. It was intended to serve as a canopy over the altar. There are many churches in different parts of England with semi circular apses. The idea was not new.

Christ Church, Panchmarhi had all of the above features, although it lacked the more stylised details. The portico and nave with their pitched roofs and gables were easily and inexpensively made and were useful for shedding water. The stone was of course procured locally. The carved timbers known as windbracers, were placed, as their name implies, to ensure that the rafters stayed in place during high winds. They run at an angle on the sides between the horizontal purlins and the vertical principal rafters The imported stained glass was obviously a novelty. It was made up of small pieces of different coloured glass that were held together by strips of lead called "cames". While their allegorical significance is relevant a more down to earth explanation is that a stained glass window, unlike a wood panelled one could not be opened in the cold weather and would therefore help to keep the interior warm! The church even accommodated a "rose" window and a square steeple with a spire, although these were supposedly later additions. Both steeple and stained glass windows are intrinsic features of a European church–their purpose being to remind the congregation to look heavenward and also to remember Christ through the allegorical stories depicted on the stained glass.

There is no record of who funded the church at Panchmarhi but it can be conjectured that the building was subsidised both by members of the congregation and the PWD. Indeed, as Dane Kennedy points out private investments were the major form of financial support for these structures.[6] For stations like Panchmarhi, the most important source of revenue was the residents themselves. Once they became legally recognised municipalities, small towns could levy all kinds of fees and taxes. There were taxes on land, buildings market stalls, servants, rickshaws, carts and other vehicles, even on horses, cows, mules and slaughtered animals. Other levies included conservancy taxes, fees for gathering firewood and grasses in municipal forests, fines for breaking municipal ordinances and octroi on goods entering municipal limits. The revenues so collected were used to maintain water supplies and other civic amenities like conservancy services, roads etc. Panchmarhi also attracted visitors as a result of these amenities and many of them made profitable investments in land and buildings.

The other church in Panchmarhi is the Anunciation Church, a Catholic place of worship started in 1921 and completed in 1925. It also has some interesting architectural features, like an Italian Marble flooring and Belgian stained glass windows. This church is still active and there is evidence of the availability of funds for its upkeep

Irwin stayed on as Executive Engineer until he was transferred to Simla in 1881. During this period, the family travelled to Panchmarhi pretty regularly, especially during the hot summer months. It was a retreat which even today attracts visitors from across the country. Fortunately, and despite the newer hotels, Panchmarhi still retains much of its countryfied character.

Notes

1. Dane Kennedy: The Magic Mountains Berkeley (University of California Press, 1996)
2. Walter Reeve The Old Cemetery at Panchmarhi (Paperback 2010)
3. Ibid
4. Ibid
5. Vikram Bhatt: Panchmarhi Church Records (Fr T. Joseph)
6. Peter Scriver ed and Vikramaditya Prakash: Colonial Modernities (Rouledge,2007)
7. James Betley: Ph.d., thesis on Late 19th Century Church Decoration (Courtald Institute, 1999)

SIMLA: VICEREGAL LODGE

CHAPTER 5

THE LODGE ON
OBSERVATORY HILL

We have already seen how the Hill Stations of India, a colonial British contribution, were, as Dane Kennedy describes them, "places where the British went to play." They were summer resorts where during the hot weather, the higher echelons of the Government of India retreated to beat the harsh hot season of the Indian plains, to govern their Indian subjects from a distance, in climes and surroundings closely resembling the home country. How much time was actually spent in the business of governance and how much in private pleasures was difficult to determine. Certainly the inaccessibility of these locations to Indians in general and the British business communities of Calcutta and Madras were plus points. The issue of these annual migrations to the hills.

stirred up much controversy and eventually led to questions raised by the Secretary of State and Parliament about their financial and political costs.

In the late 19th century, Simla had come to be designated as the summer capital of British India. Viceroys and their Councils spent at least twice as many months in Simla as they did in Calcutta, then the capital of the Raj. What the town lacked was a residence suitable for the status of a Viceroy. Previous Governor Generals and Viceroys used to lease private homes for their stay in Simla, including the mock Tudor "Peterhof", whose first occupant was James Bruce, Earl of Elgin. "Peterhof" subsequently served as the Punjab High Court and still later as the official residence of the Governor of Himachal. Today it is a 5 star hotel.

The situation was corrected after 1884 by the new incumbent, Frederick Hamilton Blackwood, 1st Marquess of Dufferin and Ava, who was appointed Viceroy of India that year. Dufferin worked closely with Henry Irwin, then Chief Superintendent of Works, Simla Circle to ensure the new building was completed before he left India in 1888. The Viceroy himself took a personal and active interest in the construction of the building.He suggested the general plan and until the designs were completed continually examined and modified the drawings in detail. He visited the construction site every morning and evening sometimes to the discomfort of the Public Works Department. Henry Irwin was the Chief Superintendent of Works but with him were Executive Engineers Hebbert and St. Clair and Assistant Engineers

Macpherson and English. The three first named had their names inscribed on the front porch. The house possessed one of the most commanding views of Simla and the neighbouring hills. It consisted of a main block of three stories with a kitchen wing at a slightly lower elevation so that from its north eastern side, including one of its corner towers, it had a lofty, somewhat forbidding appearance almost like a an English medieval castle. That this rather grim looking grey building which the Dufferins so eulogised was in fact a combination of Scottish baronial, Gothic Revival, and Jacobethan adorned with balustrades, collonades, crenellations turrets and similar other features did not seem to matter much to the incumbents. The overall effect of the exterior was not very beautiful. Inside, Irwin employed some of the traditional features of the Jacobethan style like the traditional entrance hall parallel to the portico, the long galleries the loggias facing the entrance hall and of course the grand wooden open well staircase to recreate the impression of spatial grandeur.

Dufferin's predecessor in office, Lord Ripon, had attempted certain reforms which alienated entrenched British political and economic interests while raising hopes of participation in the governance of the country, among educated Indians. Dufferin's role therefore was to try and steer a middle course between a disgruntled Anglo India and educated Indians, particularly the princely representatives of a bygone feudal India. The period of his service in India was marked among other things by important political developments such as the annexation of Upper Burma (1885-86) and mitigating the threat of a Russian invasion of Afghanistan. The first meeting of the All India Congress also took place at this time, in 1885. Despite his watchfulness of influential figures like Alan Octavian Hume in nationalist circles Dufferin preferred to remain publicly silent until very nearly the end of his Governor Generalship. On 30th November 1888 at a St. Andrews Day dinner in Calcutta, a few weeks before leaving India he delivered a speech attacking the pretensions of educated Indians whom he regarded as a "microscopic minority" of the Indian population. However he realised that the British administration in India would have to win moderate educated Indian support to survive.[1]

Dufferin's wife, Lady Harriet Dufferin accompanied her husband on his travels in India and made her own name as a pioneer in the medical training of women in India. Her extensive travel writings and photographs in addition to her medical work challenged some traditional assumptions about the role of British women in colonial life. Excerpts from her diary with accompanying full blown illustrations–some of them quite rare like the original silk scroll presented to the Dufferins in Rangoon, 1886, a handwritten letter by Dufferin and photographs of the Marchioness on horseback from the now extinct firm of Bourne and Shepherd of Calcutta and Simla–show aspects of life in India and Burma during Dufferin's Viceroyalty and provide a delightful, if somewhat rarefied window into aspects of a Vicereine's life during the Raj. Among others they contain anecdotes about the Dufferins' arrival in India, their servants, the Viceroy's houses at Calcutta

Barrackpore and Simla, native entertainment including descriptions of a typical "nautch" and visits to the zenana. In addition, Lady Dufferin's impressions of Simla in its various aspects, their travels to Delhi, Agra and Rajasthan, Lucknow, after the Uprising, the king of Awadh's gardens, Burma and Madras and accounts of various meetings with the rulers of India's Princely states and the Burmese King Thibaw, lend interesting perspectives to a period of Colonial India's history, now largely forgotten.

In 1885 concluding a visit to Rawalpindi and Lahore, Lady Dufferin visited Simla and stayed at Peterhof for the first time with her husband. Her impressions, "greatly tempered by the consideration that it is to be our home for the greater part of the year" are reproduced below for interest The account also gives a vivid description of the road to Simla

"We breakfasted early, and then started off on our long eight hour drive–D. and I in one 'victoria', the girls in another, and the rest of our party in much less comfortable machines called tongas. Yesterday was lovely and we saw the mountains looking their very best. We went at a great pace, ascending and descending, and twisting and turning round the most fearful corners, always at the edge of a precipice! Sometimes our road was exactly opposite to us, either very much higher or very much lower on the other side of a ravine; sometimes it seemed altogether lost, and was only to found again by pursuing it round some very sharp angle. There were patches of cultivation almost all the way up, culminating in beautiful and enormous rhododendron trees. For the rest the the scenery is that of a real sea of mountains, rolling hills of various heights, with snowy peaks in the distance, but no very striking range or particular peak to appeal to one's imagination. We changed horses every four miles, but even so our last pair seemed to feel the ascent to Government House very severely; indeed the road had become more precipitous and more angular than ever!

"The house itself is a cottage, and would be very suitable for any family desiring to lead a domestic and not an official life–so personally we are comfortable; but when I look around my small drawing room, and consider all the other dimunitive apartments, I do feel that it is very unfit for Viceregal establisment. Altogether it is the funniest place! At the back of the house you have about a yard to spare before you tumble down a precipice, and in front there is there is room for just one tennis court before you go over another. The A.D.C.s are all slipping off the hill in various little bungalows and go through most perilous adventures before coming to dinner. Walking, riding, driving, all seem to to me to be indulged in at the risk of one's life and even of unsafe roads there is a limited variety. I have three leading ideas on this subject of Simla at present. First I feel I have never been in such an out of the way place before; secondly, that I have never lived in such a small house; and thirdly I never saw a place so cramped in every way out of doors. I fear this last sensation will grow upon me. There is one drive which I tried to take yesterday, but had to turn back because of a thunderstorm."

Three years later, on July 15, 1888 Lady Dufferin[2] wrote about her first impressions of Simla's new Viceregal Lodge designed by Henry Irwin. It was commissioned just in time for the new Viceroy and his family to move in to their summer residence before saying their final goodbyes to this country:

"I went up to the new house this afternoon and it did look lovely. It was Simla's most beautiful moments, between showers, when clouds and hills, and light and shade all combine to to produce the most glorious effects. One could have spent hours at the window of my unfurnished boudoir, looking out on the plains in the distance, with a great river flowing through; at the variously shaped hills in the foreground, brilliantly coloured in parts and softened down in others by the fleecy clouds floating over them or nestling in the valleys between them. The approaching sunset too made the horizon gorgeous with red and golden and pale blue tints. The result of the whole was to make me feel that it is a great pity that we shall have so short a time to live in a house surrounded by such magnificent views.

"The house too now that it approaches completion, looks so well and perhaps this is a good opportunity to give you some idea of it.

The entrance hall is the great feature of it. The staircase goes up from it and there are stone pillars dividing it from a wide corridor leading to the state rooms and both hall and corridor are open to the top of the house three stories. This gives an idea of space and height which is very grand. The corridor opens into the ball room with a large arch and a similar arch at one end of the ballroom, which is a lovely room furnished with gold and brown silks and with large bow windows and a small tower recess off it. Sitting in it you look down the ball room the colouring of which is of a lighter yellow. It is a very fine room and outside the dancing space there is plenty of room for sitting as the wall is much broken up into pillars, leaving a sort of gallery round it. At one side in one of these spaces there are the large doors of the dining room. It is a beautiful room. It has a high panelling of teak along the top of which are shields with the arms and coronets of all the Viceroys and of the most celebrated Governor Generals, and above that Spanish leather in rich dark colours. The curtains are crimson. There is a small drawing room furnished in blue. These are all on one side of the hall. On the other side is the Council Room, the ADC's room, Private Secretary's office, etc.

Upstairs, the Viceroy's study and my boudoir are next to each other and my views are as I have said quite splendid. D's room is rather dark and serious looking. The colouring of mine is a bright sort of brown and it has a very large bow window and a tower room recess which is all glass like the one in the drawing room. The girls will have a similar sitting room above me and all our bedrooms are equally nice.

"The newest features of the house, as an Indian house, is the basement. Offices are almost unknown here and linen china plate and stores are accustomed to take their chance in verandahs or godowns of the roughest description. Now each has its own place and there is moreover a laundry in the house. How the dhobies will like it at first I don't know. What they are accustomed to is to squat on the brink of a cold stream and there to flog and batter our wretched garments against the hard stones until they think them clean. Now they will be condemned to warm water and soap, to mangles and ironing and drying rooms and they will probably think it all unnecessary and will perhaps faint with the heat."[3]

On July 23, 1888 she again wrote: "We really inhabit the new Viceregal Lodge today so I left the old directly after breakfast just returning there for an hour at lunch time and busied myself the whole day arranging my room and my things and the furniture in the drawing rooms. Happily the weather was very tolerable and our beds got here dry. D and the girls didn't come near the place till dinner time when everything was brilliantly lit by the electric light. It is certainly very good and the lighting up and putting out of the lamps is so simple that it is a pleasure to go round one's room touching a button here and there and to experiment with varying amounts of light. After dinner we went down to look at the kitchen which is a splendid apartment with white tiles six feet high all round the walls looking so clean and bright. We sit in the smaller drawing room which is still a little stiff and company like but it will soon get into our ways and be more comfortable.[4]

Electricity was unknown in Simla in the 1880s. Its introduction in the new Viceregal Lodge was a novelty and on the night of August 8th, the Dufferins entertained for the first time in the new house.

"We had our first entertainment in our new house tonight", wrote Lady Dufferin," It looked perfectly lovely and one could see that everyone was quite astonished at it and the softness of the light. First we had a large dinner–sixtysix people at one long table. The electric light is enough but as candelabras ornament the table we had some on it. At one end of the room there was a sideboard covered with gold plate and at the other end, double doors were open and across the ball room one one saw the band which played during dinner. . . . We had all the Council and personages of Simla and the Minister, Asman Jah from Hyderabad who brought his suite. After dinner people began to arrive for the dance. When not dancing, everyone was amused roaming about the new rooms, going upto the first floor whence they could look down on the party."[5]

Ten years later, these expressions of admiration had changed to contempt. The Curzons were not particularly happy with the place. They disparaged the building with its mock baronial porches and its pseudo feudal towers and no less the Maples furniture inside. Both the Viceroy and his wife thought that the company at dinner made them feel they were dining every day in the housekeeper's room with the butler and the lady's maid. It got so bad that they took to camping in a field near the Simla Golf Course.[6] Subsequently they initiated many changes to the exterior and interior of the building. In 1916, Secretary of State, Montague, thought it resembled a "Scottish hydro" (an electric power house) and some others felt it resembled Pentonville prison! According to another authority on English architecture the building bore a striking resemblance to Hardwick Hall in Northern England where one of the three paramours of Queen Elizabeth 1st of England kept Mary Queen of Scots in "protective custody" before she was removed to Fotheringay in 1570 and executed. Edwin Lutyens too, was critical of Simla's hybrid architecture. Commenting on the mock Tudor houses there he is reported to have said, "If one was told that the monkeys had built it, all one could only say (would be) "what wonderful monkeys–they must be shot in case they do it again!"[7] Indeed at one time a dozen men were apparently hired to keep the monkeys–a plentiful tribe even in today's Shimla–at bay from the Lodge's manicured lawns. Lutyens' sentiments have been echoed by post colonial British historians who were struck by Simla's "strange little hybrid world–part Highlands, part Himalayas; part powerhouse, part playground"[8]–this last epithet based on Rudyard Kipling's surprise "that the Viceroy and his advisers should choose to spend half the year on the wrong side of an irresponsible river" cut off from those they governed, while officers of the Raj "sweltering in their sun baked outposts" who tried to hold the country together were freely "betrayed by their wicked wives up in the hills."[9] At any rate, the Lodge, a mish-mash of styles, and not particularly original in concept, cost Rs 970,093 to build, an extravagant sum of money in the 1880s. Irwin designed and built many more public buildings in Simla, among them, the Army Headquarters and the Railway Board Building(now the State Bank of India), the Town Hall (now the Gaiety Theatre), Ripon Hospital and the Roman Catholic Church.

Indians loyal to the Raj would raise their eyebrows, but as Claire Wrathall a visitor from Britain pointed out in London's Financial Times recently, the fact remains that Irwin's masterpiece of (con)fusion–a view shared by the writer–was, in her opinion, one of the ugliest buildings of the Raj. An important consideration no doubt was that the locals had never seen or heard of Jacobethan or Elizabethan architecture before. It did not much matter to them what style was adopted and by whom, as long as it provided employment. Indeed it is significant that in the 19th century, there was a significant increase in the number of workmen employed for PWD projects not to speak of porterage and other services for British visitors to the hills. Much of this workforce was recruited from surrounding villages but retinues of *khitmatgars, khansamas* and *ayahs* also followed their masters so that they would be well looked after during the long summer season. There was large scale exploitation both in terms of labour and wages. Some of the stone used in building the new Viceregal Lodge had to be carried manually, uphill and on foot, from quarries, some as far as 50km away. In view of the fact that Indians were actively discouraged from visiting this most hallowed of British preserves–Curzon was outraged to learn that a Bengali zamindar had purchased a house in Simla–the locals meekly accepted the new edifice as a monument to the British presence and the Colonial Government's intention to project its unconcealed superiority over an "inferior" race.

Notes

1. Lady Harriet Dufferin: Our Viceregal Life in India, London (John Murray 1889)

2. Ibid

3. Ibid

4. Ibid

5. Ibid

6. Niall Ferguson: Empire: (Allen Lane and Penguin, London 2003)

7. T. Metcalf: An Imperial Vision Berkeley (University of California Press 1989)

8. A Tradition Created (History Today Vol.32 No.9 1962)

9. Op. Cit

MADRAS: THE LAW COURTS:
A FOREST OF ONION SHAPED
DOMES TO CROWN A VICTORIAN MOORISH BUILDING

CHAPTER 6

EXUBERANCE, IMITATION AND COMPROMISE

By the time Henry Irwin arrived in Madras armed with his new portfolio as Consulting Architect to the Government, his predecessor, Robert Fellowes Chisholm, had already left. Chisholm was one of the pioneers of the Indo Saracenic movement in the city and had initiated several projects in that style. It fell to Henry Irwin to carry on the tradition created by his predecessor. The debate about whether the Indo Saracenic movement that included Indian elements should be projected as a concession to the subject country with British postures as natural successors to the Mughals, or whether they represented a boast of British mastery over India's cultural past, was continuing. Already in 1873 the British Parliament had recorded a statement made by a senior member of the

Civil Service who claimed that the colonial administrative structure in India was no more than a "temporary" arrangement. He compared it to a scaffolding "which has been erected until the edifice of our Empire is completed." "And as it is completed", he continued, "that scaffolding should be taken down."[1] In the same year, T. Roger Smith addressing the Royal Society of Arts in London was emphatic that "meddling with Eastern styles was simply "un-British."[2] He is reported to have said "We ought like the Romans and the Mahommedans to take our national style with us . . . we shall be likely to succeed best if we are not too anxious to incorporate much of the art or style of the country with our own."[3]

The engineer dominated Public Works Department, which Irwin represented had, by this time, run dry of designs other than the purely utilitarian. As the quintessential engineer turned architect, it made sense to use these designs as basic infrastructures to which domes and minarets could be added to give them an "oriental" look. The PWD was an essentially British institutionalised agency specialising in the building of law courts, government offices, schools, colleges, clubs railway stations police stations, jails cantonments and many other such structures which would help project British dominance over civil society at the time. However there were other considerations.

James Fergusson, whose History of Indian and Eastern Architecture (1876) is considered to be the first comprehensive account of the growth and development of Indian architecture, outlined a theory which sought to divide

Indian building traditions and patterns based on religious and racial divisions. In his view, there were distinct differences between the Aryan/Dravidian and Sanskritic/non Sanskritic cultures. These accounted for the stylistic variations between "Hindu" and "Muhammedan" architecture and, to quote Fergusson, "the mediocre intellectual status" of the South Indians. According to him, "In the south, civil architecture as a fine art is quite extinct and though sacred architecture still survives in a certain queer, quaint form of temple building, it is of so low a type that it would hardly be a matter of regret if it too ceased to exist and the curtain dropped over the graves of both, as they are arts that practically have become extinct."[4] Therefore, Fergusson argued, the decisive marker of Indian architectural antiquity was its Aryan or North Indian racial pedigree[5] Another pioneer of the movement, Emerson, argued that Islamic architecture in India was "notable for its adaptation to local conditions,"[6] To add insult to injury, the term Indo Saracenic—a style subsequently initiated by Benfield, Chisholm and Irwin—to reflect and vindicate that pedigree, was also inappropriate if not incorrect. The Saracens, a tribe in Arabia outside the pale of European and/ or Mughal influence had no relevance to India, In the context of Mughal architecture the description was simplistic if not distinctly derisive.

British colonial engineers obviously acquiesced in these uninformed and outlandish views, and the absence of any recorded treatises of South India's secular Hindu vernacular architectural heritage helped. Other than the great temple complexes which were the equivalent of public buildings in medieval India, civil life revolved round these complexes and royal palaces. Residential buildings like the Agraharams, incorporating verandahs and courtyards, were few and far between. Additionally, Irwin's South Indian associates had no contribution to make to the debate. They chose to remain silent and accepted to share the white man's views provided it brought material benefits. An Indian master builder of the time, a close associate of Irwin, Thattikonda Namberumal Chetty, acquired as many as ninety nine properties in his lifetime. In the manner set by his mentor, Chetty had a stable with fine horses and was the first Indian to own a motor car. Many more honours came his way, such as titles like Rao Sahib and Dewan Bahadur not to speak of membership of the Madras Legislative Council and a Bank Directorship.

Henry Irwin's name is associated with a number of monuments in old Madras, not all of them beautiful or spectacular, but they represent a period of Indian architectural history. They were a novelty, and reflected the incapability of their designers to assimilate the ethos of prior historic models. Given the stylistic limitations of hybridity, the risks inherent in such projects for persons like Irwin, without formal architectural training, were formidable. The new colonial builders and their Indian associates genuinely believed that by enhancing the physical configuration of the built environment, social and moral improvement of the subject race was possible. The rhetoric of cultural commitment, gave the movement sufficient impetus to warrant public interest. All that can be said about these buildings is that the concept was an ingenious, if unrealistic one.

In 1889 Irwin underook his first project in Madras–The High Court and Law College– displayed on the cover of this book. Irwin needed to share the distinction with one J.N.Brassington. who is supposed to have prepared the original designs. However, the construction was entrusted to Namberumal Chetty under the supervision of Engineer J.H. Stephen. With their high ceilings, ornamental tiling stained glass arches grillework and tall minaret, (possibly the tallest in Madras) they have been described as "beautiful" and "imposing."[7] A less enthusiastic observer commented that they were "comparatively pedestrian" with the "painted brickwork and massing of this enormous range following the Public Works Department's standard utilitarian formula" except for the towers and roofline which helped to turn them "Oriental." In 1894. a powerful flashing light was installed on the minaret to act as the city's third lighthouse. The winding open staircase to access the lamp was perhaps a little uncharitably described by the same commentator as "disturbingly reminiscent of a Piranesi dungeon."[8]

But perhaps the most graphic description of this incredible monument is found in the following lines by Jan Morris: "This huge red sandstone building challenges description, so splendidly jumbled was its presence, so elaborate were its forms, so complex and disturbing its effects . . . next door to the courts stood the Law College and every traveller arriving by sea to Madras saw the buildings before they disembarked, for they stood on the Esplanade, a little away from the docks;and with their multitudinous towers, pinnacles and domes, some brightly coloured, some decorated in stucco patterns, they presented a terrifically fanciful welcome to the city, in grandiose partnersip with the classical restraint of Fort St George. After commenting on the "contrapuntal" and "cryptlike" surprises in the building "court after court, staircase after staircase, warrens of vaulted corridors, half hidden alcoves and huge verandahs" the writer concludes her observations by remarking that the last "symbolic construction" by Messrs Irwin and Stephens was a "bulbous and eccentric tower with an unsuitably phallic look."[9]

Another Irwin project was to develop the complex known as the Pantheon, a name derived from their earlier use as the "Public Assembly Rooms", where among others, Cornwallis and Wellesley were feted following their respective victories over Tipu Sultan (1799) and the Marathas at Assaye (1803). The complex was originally a place of public entertainment and balls and subsequently rechristened the "Collector's Cutchery". It houses an old museum with a red brick rotunda surrounded by an Italianate arcade and the well known Connemara Library. Connemara, a philanderer of sorts, was something of a controversial figure and did not perhaps deserve to be remembered in this way At any rate the library

MADRAS: THE CONNEMARA LIBRARY WITH
ITS SEMI CIRCULAR ITALIANATE FRONT AND
AN OCTAGONAL TOWER TOPPED WITH
A RAJASTHANI TYPE CHHATRI

MADRAS: VICTORIA MEMORIAL TO LOOK LIKE
AKBAR'S BULAND DARWAZA IN FATEHPUR SIKRI

was formally opened in 1896. It was built by Namberumal Chetty, but the interior with its ornamental wooden ceiling, copies of antique wooden furniture stained glass and mullioned windows and superimposed ornamental columns reminiscent of English Tudor/Elizabethan/Jacobean elements–was fashioned by Irwin. Around this time Irwin also began work on the headquarters of the Imperial Bank of India (now the State Bank of India) in company with Namberumal Chetty, in the same mixture of styles, and the new functional and decorative Egmore Station, incorporating traditional Tamil motifs with typical 19th century arches and vaulted roofs, with Master builder T. Samynada Pillai. The Irwin Pavilion at the Madras Cricket Club (since demolished) and a Gujarati Jeweller's showroom on Mount Road (Anna Salai), also since demolished, were his other projects. Once again Namberumal Chetty was the principal contractor and builder.

One of Irwn's best recognised works was of course the Victoria Memorial Hall designed first as the headquarters of the Victoria Technical Institute and now known as the Art Gallery in Madras (1907). Not to be confused with Colonial Calcutta's Victoria Memorial, it incorporates a façade borrowed from Akbar's Buland Darwaza at Fatehpur Sikri. The building was a faithful copy in miniature of that spectacular Mughal monument, complete with scalloped battlements, slim minarets and chhatris and built with the red sandstone of North India. The difference was that like most other PWD constructions the building was set up on an elevated plinth with a brick and mortar framework to imitate the high ridge on which the original stands. It was built to honour Queen Victoria on her Golden Jubilee but apart from serving a political purpose, the building was strangely out of place in Dravidian Tamil Nadu. Akbar never ruled South India. His Buland Darwaza was built to commemorate the Mughal Emperor's victory over Gujerat. The original Buland Darwaza or Victory Gate with its Quranic inscriptions, a major tourist attraction for visitors to Fatehpur Sikri, opens out into the courtyard of Akbar's capital city and its mosque. While Irwin's attention to detail in creating a near identical copy was commendable and doubtless found favour with his employers, it was certainly not an example of creative excellence or originality.

Comparatives have been drawn between the public buildings of colonial Madras, and Calcutta. A few examples to illustrate the essentials should suffice to highlight the differences. Calcutta was basically an extension of the Sunderbans. It was a city described by early travellers like William Hodges as "a collection of handsome buildings, on a mud flat surrounded by gardens. Others like Lord Valentia and Maria Graham remarked that it was "an entire village of palaces" and indeed on the general appearance of "grandeur" in all its buildings." Poets too extolled the virtues of the city, describing Calcutta as "the pomp of spires and palaces" or "the little London in Bengal . . . a wonder formed like island on the main, amidst a sea of pagans." In an age when there were no cameras, the only recorded evidence of these observations were the work of a large number of British landscape artists who started coming to India in the last quarter of the 18th century, notably painters like William Hodges, Thomas and William Daniell, James Moffat, Francois Solvyns, Charles Doyly, James Bailley Fraser, William Havell, William Prinsep George Chinnery and many others. Their drawings vividly captured the polished white Palladian buildings of Calcutta with flat or balustrated roofs, set against a clear blue cloudless sky, merchant ships sailing up the Hooghly and the dark green vegetation of the city–a combination totally new to an Englishman accustomed to the damp and fog of his native country.

It will be obvious from the foregoing that much of Calcutta's architecture, particularly in the White Town, consisted of imitation Neo Classical or Palladian styles popular in England during that period. In 18th century Calcutta, as it is today in Mumbai and elsewhere, landed property was a lucrative business.Building costs were high, as basic building materials like brick stone and durable wood had to be imported from outside the city.Consequently rents were exhorbitant and 'pukka' (masonry) buildings were fruitful investments. Only a few wealthy inhabitants could afford the luxury of a large house in a spacious garden. There was no dearth of these among the British merchants who according to the Calcutta Gazette of 1806 made immense fortunes by the purchase and sale of expensive artefacts like jewelled armour, Arab stallions, European built coaches, engravings, paintings and expensive furniture. As English women were a rarity in India at the time it was also common practice for a European bachelor to take on a Eurasian or an Indian mistress on arrival in Calcutta. There are stories of horses, carriages, palanquins and whole housefuls of servants and retainers to attend to the new arrival. Such were the symbols of gentility if not also a necessary part of it. It will be appreciated that many of these mansions served as offices and private residences.

The British obsession with classification, division and separation led to elaborate artifices of delimitation such as wrought iron railings and gates, masonry walls and elaborate gateways as an extension of the architecture of the main building. They functioned as preparatory devices of what was to be found inside—more often than not, a house with pillared verandahs, a flat roof surrounded by a light collonaded balustrade and a front relieved by a deep portico supported by lofty columns. The buildings with rare exceptions were oriented with their long axes running north-south allowing for carriage ports to the north and verandahs on the south to catch the summer breeze. While internal layouts differed, they typically consisted of several sets of rooms, one set on the axis with the carriage port and south verandah and two sets of rooms on either side thus creating a three bay pattern. The hall was the principal entrance and gathering space in the colonial house. Due to the scarcity of public places for accommodation and recreation, there was a need to provide for large gatherings. Typically breakfasts brought 15 people to the table and dinner, 25. In fact, contrary to their British counterparts, all of the spaces in earlier colonial Calcutta houses had multiple uses. It was a method of responding to a changing market in which there was no assurance that the building would continue in its present use.[10]

Mention has already been made of Calcutta's Government House, built by the Marquis of Wellesley after John Adams' design of Kedleston Hall in England.One of Calcutta's first public buildings, the Town Hall, a structure described by the British columnist Desmond Doig as "a building of generous and elegant proportions" was built in the Neo Classical style by one John Garstin a Colonel in the Corps of British Engineers in 1813. Belvedere House (now the National Library) was built in the Italian Renaissance style. From 1769 it became the country seat of the British Governors of Bengal and later, the winter residence of visiting Viceroys to Calcutta. The well known Boys' School, La Martiniere, had a dome supported by Corinthian pillars which once housed a chapel, consecrated in 1836. Hastings House in Alipore. Calcutta's General Post Office, Prinsep Ghat Metcalfe Hall, the Asiatic Society and many more, were all a part of the Palladian or British Neo Classical architectural style popular in the period. Fort William itself boasted of fine buildings in that style, namely the house occupied by Lord Kitchener of Khartoum and the old Government House

Calcutta also had its share of hybrid buildings. Indian imitations of these mansions until well into the 19th century were a mixture of styles. For want of a better terminology they were derided as "Ballygunge Baroque" or "Shyambazar Victoriana". They indicate that regardless of proportions, the new language of neo classicism was adopted (a) because it was fashionable and (b) because the Bengali elite were eager to follow their political superiors. Besides, Calcutta's High Court, for instance, a replica it is said, of the Staad Haus at Ypres, boasts a tall belfry, pointed Moorish arches and foliated pillars. It stands in stark contrast to the Town Hall next door. Like some of Madras' heritage buildings, it has been vandalised by contractors who believe that they have added "improvements" to the original. The red brick sprawl of the Sir Stuart Hogg Market (better known as the New Market) is representative of late Victorian architecture complete with Victorian wrought iron beams and a timeless Clock tower reminiscent of some Indo Saracenic buidings in South India, like the Moore Market. Likewise, there were elements of hybridity–some quite bizarre–in many of Calcutta's prominent landmarks, built by the Tagore family, like the Tagore Castle with turrets, which remind us of Balmoral or the Baitakkhana designed by a French architect or Vijay Manzil the Calcutta residence of the Maharajas of Burdwan a combination of "Gothic, Corinthian, Colonial and Mackintosh Burn"[11]. All of these contributed to the architecture of the city until the British decided to shift their capital to New Delhi in 1911.

The Bombay comparative is even more curious. The rivalry between Calcutta and Bombay, the two outposts of Empire was reflected in entirely different architectural styles. The latter–its public buildings a strange concoction of Moorish domes and Gothic, jumbled with pitched roofs, Victorian buttresses, gargoyles and turrets–have drawn both admiration and severe criticism, very often leaving informed visitors wondering about the extent of Bombay's "Westernisation." Unlike Calcutta, many British residential bungalows of Bombay were, in the initial years, made of wood. Some drew their inspiration from the many tiered wooden Gujerati houses of which Bombay can still provide examples. Garden houses, not necessarily in the grand manner of Calcutta, first began to appear in the 18th century as suburban European bungalows set among the shore plantations north of the Esplanade, on the old Mazagaon estate and along the shore of Back Bay. These borrowed styles from Medieval European cities like overhanging wooden balconies and projecting eaves. The result of all these closely built wooden houses was of course the disastrous fire of 1803 which accounted for their eventual disappearance. One of the reasons why Bombay was so different was that it was never a full fledged colonial city like Calcutta. Its Anglo Indian infrastructure was geared mainly to meet a floating population of Europeans who used Bombay as a stopping off point on their way to other parts of India and/ or to strike commercial deals, not excluding its shipyards, which under the stewardship of Parsees like Jamshetji Bomanji Wadia supplied warships of unbeatable quality to the British Government such as the one that fought at the Battle of Trafalgar.

Overall, the Madras experiment, like other architectural fantasies of the period, was an exercise in invoking popular support for an alien government while at the same time imposing an umistakeably English flavour on these creations. Those among the local population who were given the opportunity of serving the colonial administrattion in postions of privilege were suitably brainwashed to function as interpreters of European values. Unfortunately these attitudes persist. It may be some years before they can be discarded in favour of an appropriate secular domestic and public architecture culturally rooted but politically neutral Eastern tradition. The other question which comes to mind is how many people actually notice their architectural surroundings. I have not come across many Indians who do and certainly none who question the credentials of their creators or their motivations. The architectural history of Colonial India is replete with gushing descriptions by locals of the creations of the ruling power. Ironically, we seem to have left critical thinking and analysis about these creations to others. The work of those Indians who in the last ten years have made it their business to carve a niche for themselves in this emerging space of architectural inquiry therefore, deserve to be carried with acclaim.

Notes

1. T. Roger Smith "Architectural Art in India" (Journal of the Society of Arts, 1873 Vol 21 March 7)
2. Ibid
3. Ibid
4. James Fergusson: History of Indian and Eastern Architecture (Dodd Mead & Co, London 1899)
5. Ibid

6. Ibid

7. S.Muthiah: Madras Rediscovered (Chennai, Westland Limited, 2008)

8. Giles Tillotson: Architectural Styles in British India 1837-1910 (Marg vol 46 No1, 1994)

9. Jan Morris: Stones of Empire (Oxford University Press 1983, pg 114)

10. Swati Chattopadhyay: Modernity, Nationalism and the Colonial Uncanny (Routledge, 2006)

11. Desmond Doig: Calcutta: An Artist's Impression (The Statesman. Commercial Printing Press, Calcutta)

MYSORE: AMBA VILAS PALACE:

A LITTLE BIT OF EVERYTHING

CHAPTER 7

A PALACE LIKE NO OTHER

The royal palace of Mysore was, for several centuries the home of the Wodeyar rulers who were the vassals of the Vijaynagar kings. The Wodeyars ruled Mysore from 1399 until 1947 except for a brief interregnum of 38 years when Haider Ali and his son Tipu Sultan ruled Mysore. In 1793 Tipu Sultan razed the old city and rebuilt it as we see it today with obvious additions through the colonial era. Palace records and archives show that since the 14th century the Wodeyars lived in what was essentially a wooden structure surrounded by a jumble of ordinary homes quite close to it. In 1638 the palace was struck by lightning and rebuilt by Kantirava Narasa Raja Wodeyar (1638-1659) who also added to the existing structure by adding new pavilions. His successor Chikka Devaraja Wodeyar who operated out of Seringapatam, the new capital of the state, annexed several new territories during his lifetime. Between these two rulers, Mysore was transformed into a powerful state in the Southern Deccan. In the latter half of the 18th century Mysore came into conflict with the Marathas, the British and the Nizam of Golconda leading to the Anglo Mysore Wars and eventually, to Tipu Sultan's death in 1799. The kingdom's territories were distributed by the British to their allies and the landlocked kingdom of Mysore headed by a scion of the Wodeyar family was reinstated as the puppet monarch of a princely state under the suzerainty of the British crown. Krishnaraja Wodeyar III was only five when he was annointed king.The coronation ceremony took place under a marquee. On coming of age, one of his first tasks was to rebuild the palace of his ancestors. Unfortunately, in 1897 the hastily built palace was razed to the ground by a fire at the wedding of Princess Jayalakshmanni. The Queen Regent, Maharani Vannivilasa Sannidhana then decided to commission Henry Irwin to build a new palace, known as the Amba Vilas, on the foundations of the old one. The work was completed in 1912. at a cost of Rs 41,47,913. In Irwin's honour the road connecting Mysore Railway Station to the present Mysore KSRTC Bus Stand is named Irwin Road.

The reasons behind the Maharani's decision are not far to seek. The young Maharaja of Mysore was the just the kind of person the British, especially Curzon, had in mind. He was educated by a senior ICS man, Sir Stuart Fraser and his Private Secretary, a man by the name of Evan Machonochie, who was also drawn from that service. The Maharaja was duly guided in the Western way of doing things—clearing slums, straightening and widening roads putting a new drainage system in place and generally "tidying up." Niall Fergusson describes the "playboy Maharaja" as "wealthy, Westernised and weakened to the point of political impotence"—the type who was to become a familiar figure throughout India.[1]

The main features of the new palace described by an eye witness Aline Dobbie, were its huge ornamental gateways in front of the palace and several smaller edifices within its walled compound. The area in front of the palace behind the boundary resembled "a large manicured parade ground." I crave permission to quote extensively from her book,[2] one of the finest accounts of the palace interiors that I have read:

Dobbie starts with a description of the five temples in the palace grounds which predate the palace, including the Lakshmiramana and the Varahaswami Temple. She divides the palace into two parts, the first, a "very richly decorated Public Durbar Hall (Diwan-i-Am) over 47 metres long and over 13 metres wide with gold and turqoise decoration." She describes the paintings by Raja Ravi Varma noted for his paintings of the royals, on the walls and takes us on a tour of the Private Durbar Hall (Diwan-khas) which is smaller but "as sumptuous and more intricate and delicate."[3] According to Dobbie, the Marriage pavilion or Kalyana Mandapa has a glass ceiling with stained glass imported from Glasgow and columns of triple iron cast iron and arches all made and imported from Walter Macfarlane Saracen Iron foundry also from Glasgow. Called the Peacock Pavilion all glass decorations and the mosaic floor are the peacock designed by local artists. The walls of the Pavilion are covered with murals depicting the Mysore Dussehra.

Returning to the main archway mentioned above, she describes how it opens to a wide passage (elephant gate) that finally leads to the expansive central court. Visitors are not allowed to enter through this way. The elephant gate is typically kept closed, barring ceremonial functions in the palace. The court mentioned above is open to the sky and an enclosed verandah runs around it. At regular intervals are giant window openings to the court. Also at the three sides of the open court are porches to enter the verandah. Although the porches are inaccessible, it is possible to get a good view of them through the windows. They are netted at the top to prevent birds messing the inside. Flanking the main porch are a set of giant lion images casted out of brass.

The Kalyana Mandapa which Dobbie mentions, is an octagonal open hall and brightly decorated. "Especially noteworthy are the floor tiles, the balconies, the slender cast iron pillars and the tinted glass ceiling."[4] She draws attention to the period ceiling fans here (Mysore city got its first electricity supply in 1908) and describes the whole superstructure of this octagonal shaped ceiling as having been specially made by the legendary Scottish foundry Walter MacFarlane & Co. Ltd. The tinted glasses making a peacock theme over the ceiling were brought from Belgium.

Each year the Mysore royals routinely celebrate Dussehra, a spectacular pageant held to mark the end of the Navaratri festival. The festival originated in the 15th century to mark the victory of truth over evil with the Goddess Chamundeshwari (another name for Durga) slaying the Demon Mahishasura. The occasion is marked by a public Durbar, procesions of richly caparisoned elephants, camels and courtiers and the illumination of the Royal palace. Dobbie describes the festival through the large oil paintings depicting the Mysore Dussehra which hang on the walls of the open hall. Each of the 26 paintings' theme is a function or ceremony related to Dussehra. The images are properly labelled so that visitors get can get an idea of the pomp with which it was and still is, held.She surmises that the very intention of including such paintings in the palace was to educate visitors about the history and culture of the State. Another remarkable feature in the ground floor of the palace are the pillars, the squinch (where the pillar meets the ceiling) and the domical ceiling above the verandah. A great deal of plaster work is visible on the ceiling, the capitals are beautifully carved with hard granite and the whole is a present blend of native and gothic styles.

Apart from these features Dobbie feels that palace effectively displays some of the best local traditions of craftsmanship, especially in the woodwork. She cites the massive doors carved out of teak (yellow-brown) and rosewood (coffee colored). On the rosewood doors, frames and lintels she points to the finely done inlay work which seem to look like intricate paintings, but on closer examination, turn out to be ivory chips embedded onto the surface of the rosewood. To protect tampering such inlay works are protected with transparent perplex overlay. This kind of craftsmanship can also be seen in the ceiling of the Durbar Hall and compare well with any other palace in India.

On the first floor there are two major halls. One is for the public hall and the other is a private audience hall. These can be accessed by means of a mechanical lift. The first of these, the Diwan-e-Am, or the Hall of Public Audience is a huge open hall along the width of the palace on the first floor. The eastern side is open and gives a panoramic view of the garden in front of the palace. The rows of massive pillars are the special attraction of this hall. On the south and north of the eastern portion are the galleries for the courtiers.On the western wall of the Durbar Hall is a row of paintings. Most of it is mythical themes from the Hindu pantheon.

The other, the Hall of Private Audience called Ambavilasa or the Diwan-e-Khas is the most decorative of all the areas in the palace. This is where the golden Throne of Mysore is positioned. It is unlikely that anyone would find the throne in the hall unless that person happened to visit the palace during the days of Dussehra festival. Otherwise the throne is kept in safe custody.

This hall has an intricately designed tinted glass ceiling which illuminates the hall lavishly. This light play does wonders on the otherwise brightly painted pillared Durbar Hall.On the floor, between the pillars are the embedded inlay work–Pietra dura–that is popularly known as Agra work. Various bright semiprecious stones are embedded on the marble flooring to create interesting motifs. One can see a great deal of this work on the Taj Mahal at Agra. As mentioned earlier, the ceiling around this portion has some massive and boldly executed woodwork in teak.

One of the most important architectural features of the palace is its gateways and the walls. The one located at the east is the largest of the four gateways. Between the gateways and the palace is a sprawling garden which is home to a number of temples dotted around the palace campus. The living palace where the family live is located right behind the main palace. This too is a museum exhibiting a number of artifacts used in the palace. The author feels this gives a more human and traditional touch to the exhibits. Besides providing an insight into the life of those times.

Because the earlier palace was destroyed by fire, the new one had to be fireproof. This was obviously a "modern" innovation as were the stone and metal used for the superstructures instead of the traditional woodwork. So was the lift from the ground to the first floor of the palace. Most of the palace was made of hard granite brought from quarries around the present day Mysore district, notably the stone brought from the quarries of Turuvekere in Tumkur. The workforce was pan Indian, which accounts for the mixture of styles, from the south of India, to Jaipur, Kolhapur and even Agra.

Another firsthand account of the architecture of the palace is by William G Burn Murdoch, a Scottish painter, travel writer and explorer (1862-1939) who visited Mysore in 1905.[4]

Murdoch writes

"Mysore town is a place of wide roads and trees, fields
intended to be parks some day, and light and air.Many
houses of European origin, somewhat suggestive of Italian
or Spanish villas, are shuttered and closed in, so as to
give a sense of their being deserted. You drive past these
silent houses and their gardens and come to the native
town, which is anything but silent or deserted, and then
to the new palace; the modern sight of southern India. It is
brimming with life . . . ."

Murdoch visited Mysore when the palace was being
constructed. He describes it as "a Gothic cathedral in course
of construction. Two towers, each at a guess, 150 feet high,
with a wing between them, bristle with bamboo scaffolding so
warped and twisted out of the perpendicular that the uprights
are like old fishing rods.The extraordinary intricacy is quite
fascinating . . .

"As we see it, in the afternoon, the great mass of building
is grey against the western light; thousands of men, women,
boys, and children are scattered over its face on these fragile
perches, and though not in sunlight, their many-coloured
draperies reflect on the variously coloured stones at which
they are carving."

Murdoch does not venture to give an opinion about the
overall architecture of the palace but is obviously impressed

by the skill of the craftsmen and is full of praise for the encouragement given to them by the Mysore royals.

He is equally impressed with the the variety of materials used in its construction.

"Anything from teak wood, to marble, to granite to ivory is used in tasteful ways to make this a charming piece of art; that is that the palace was not made following a standard architectural school. Rather it was generous in borrowing from various art forms—both Indian and foreign." Indeed the richness of the materials employed prompts him to compare the palace with the legendary Temple of Solomon—a palace with "marble-work and wood-work, silver doors, ivory doors, and rooms, halls, and passages . . . all carved with Indian minuteness and delicacy, with telling scenes from the stories of Hindoo deities." Albeit in good humor, Murdoch goes on to comment on the cast iron pillars:

". . . . and in the middle of these Eastern marvels are alas! cast-iron pillars from Glasgow. They form a central group from base to top of the great tower; between them at each flat they are encircled with cast-iron perforated balconies. They are made to imitate Hindoo pillars with all their taperings and swellings, and are painted vermilion and curry-colour. Opening on to these cast-iron balconies are the silver and ivory rooms and floors of exquisite marble inlay."

Clearly, neither of these observers had any intention of offending Indian sensibilities nor did they wish to deride the motives, concept or designs created by one of their own countrymen. There is no argument, I think, that Irwin's creation was pure fantasy. He had a generous budget and the architecture had a bit of everything from Islamic domes to Hindu pillars, besides tons of imported wrought iron extravagances, granite, marble, silver and ivory. Virtually every inch of wall pillar or ceiling was covered with frescoes, carvings, oil paintings and coloured (stained) glass. The overall effect was mind boggling. It was different from the architectural muddle of Simla's Viceregal Lodge and in many ways as extraordinarily outlandish, even beautiful in a way. However it is doubtful if this assemblage of a variety of Islamic type domes of all shapes and sizes–some of them pink, and others gilded–and Hindu elements like towers, chhatris, even a sculpture of the Goddess Gajalakshmi above the central arch, achieved much beyond a cross between the Prince Regent's pleasure palace by the sea in Brighton, England, and something out of an Arabian Nights' fairy tale. Looking at the palace, all that can be said of its exotic character is that we are impressed by its bold scale and detail. It was relevant in the context of its time, having replaced a rather shabby wooden structure surrounded by modest settlements. The statement therefore that "if you are poor beauty matters less" is probably not quite true. Indeed, every one of us likes gardens, wide open spaces and impressive looking buildings especially if they add value to the neighbourhood. The new palace undoubtedly created that kind of ambience. As to it's aesthetics opinions vary.

In England for example, architectural styles consistently correspond to building types, be they banks, commercial houses or universities. Likewise mid century English churches built on the principles of Perpendicular or Decorated Gothic reflected theological differences between the Oxford and Cambridge movements. Indeed, it has been argued that symbolism is essential to meaningful architecture and that the model from a previous time or from the existing city is a part of the source material of the creative architect. Irwin's Mysore palace tried unsuccessfully to capture some of this symbolism and failed. Instead he was caught up in the innovative engineering structures of the 19th century, and with inspiration pouring in from all corners of India, he seems to have indulged in an expressionism that was largely meaningless or irrelevant. To what extent he was influenced by his earlier experiments in Madras is difficult to assess. Unfortunately, this kind of architecture, though not at Irwin's level of fantasy or the Mysore royal family's level of expenditure, seems to have flourished throughout the greater part of the century.

Notes

1. Niall Fergusson: Empire, (Penguin, Allen Lane, London 2003)
2. Aline Dobbie: The Elephant's Blessing (Melrose Books, Cambridgeshire, 2006)
3. Ibid
4. William G. Burn Murdoch: Chronicles of British India (Asiatic Society Journal)

MYSORE: AMBA VILAS PALACE VIEW FROM THE FRONT

CHAPTER 8

THE IMPACT OF ENGINEERING

Notwithstanding the debate about an architectural style appropriate to the ruling class and its mastery over India's cultural past as natural successors to the Mughals, the British Parliament in 1873 recorded a statement made by a senior member of the Civil Service who claimed that the colonial administrative structure in India was no more than a "temporary" arrangement. He compared it to a scaffolding "which has been erected until the edifice of our Empire is completed." "And as it is completed", he continued, "that scaffolding should be taken down."[1] The statement, which, in a way foresaw the decline and fall of the British Empire in India also underscored the sense of "desolation" of the expatriate in an alien environment, particularly among the bureaucracy, the army and other professions. Partly to assuage these feelings and partly also to regulate the building norms of East India Company engineers in the scattered territories occupied by that organisation, the Government decided to establish the Public Works Department (PWD) which, it was hoped, would cater to varying levels in the administration and provide the infrastructure necessary for good government. Henry Irwin and his colleagues were, of course, part of that system.

The Public Works Department came into existence in 1855, two years before the Uprising of 1857. It was conceived as the formal building agency of the colonial regime in the last century of its existence. Prior to the establishment of the PWD, British building in colonial India was subject to varying degrees of autonomy and technology in the territories occupied by the East India Company, impeding uniformity in government buildings and other public spaces. PWD buildings, familiar to observers of colonial architecture in the late nineteenth and early twentieth centuries, were stylised, stereotypical and utilitarian. They were intended to serve a specific purpose, such as residences, railway stations, offices, clubs, cantonments, bridges and many others, suited to an itinerant ruling class required to move from one metropolitan city to another or from one district to another, as circumstances dictated. These prosaic, commonplace buildings portrayed, more vividly than anything else, the British penchant for order in an otherwise unfamiliar environment and their apathy to transport themselves their houses and modes of life to India, except for a term of a few years. During these periods, when some of them virtually camped here, matters of architectural substance seemed less than important, as were utilities like electricity and water as long as these could be arranged manually. The PWD drew up blueprints for virtually everything. A typical district town was divided into communities including the white, black and Eurasian communities. The railway station, the European style offices and public buildings, cantonments and parks even the district church, all conformed to set patterns which even today are instantly recognizeable. The typical bungalow for example had large rooms, plain whitewashed walls, and a wide verandah running round the house which led through in the front into a living room with bedrooms on either side, a dining room also flanked by bedrooms and bathrooms and a pantry at the back usually separated from the main kitchen which stood by itself behind the bungalow near the servants' quarters. There were templates for civil government offices, officers' mess houses for personnel in the British infantry and cavalry regiments and railway stations with staff quarters graded according to rank. Although there were local variations to suit climatic conditions the overall impression associated with PWD buildings was that they were functional and uniformly standard in design.

The PWD's building efforts in this country in the second half of the nineteenth century—developing an extensive network of roads, railways and irrigation canals, not to speak of post and telegraph offices, law courts and jails—was, of course, impressive. However, typical PWD constructions drew a slew of disparaging remarks from contemporaries. We have already seen how Major J.G. Medley, Principal of the Thomason College of Engineering, described a typical

PWD church.[2] Another critic described PWD architecture as "protesting against everything architectural, aesthetic or useful, designed and built according to a Government prescription."[3] However, if the opinions of a section of the British bureaucracy about PWD engineering and technology was derogatory, the Department came through to many others as the Government's efficient technical arm to provide accommodation and other facilities to the community at large and at all levels. Indeed, modern building technology which the PWD ushered into this country was a direct offshoot of the Industrial Revolution in England and Europe.

PWD designs and techniques were never cast as part of colonial India's revivalist architecture. However, the impact of modern engineering techniques and mechanisation on British Indian colonial architecture, including later Indo Saracenic buildings, was palpable. In a essay on the Public Works Department of British India, Peter Scriver writes about the "shifts and slippages" in the modes of design reasoning within the PWD system, from the strategic rationality of mid nineteenth century problem solving to the "make-do" and "make-believe" irrationalities of Imperial architectural representation.[4] PWD engineers like Henry Irwin, rose to become Consulting Architects on the basis of Viceregal and Princely patronage not because of his sensitivity to the Indian cultural landscape. Like many others before and after him he was given a mandate to build urbane new public buildings in cities like Madras and Mysore to develop a modern (European) architecture with a free style applique of Indian ornamentation and structural forms on the basis of mechanistic drawings and generic plans prepared for modern European public buildings such as colleges, hopitals and courthouses. They were at best, superficial examples of an authentic Indian style. Typical construction details to resemble traditional Indian motifs were circulated to Government engineers as manuals of standard practice and procedures. Likewise the technically progressive use of reinforced concrete vaulting, and other raw materials such as iron and glass, gradually replaced traditional methods of building. As Paul Walker observes, it was a "middling form of modernism that reflected a certain understanding of both the material and representational function of architecture in the colonial-modern context but could make no claim to be a genuine fusion between modern European and Indian architectures."[5] He also makes the point that the Indo Saracenics were instructed to follow Islamic designs not because of their rationality or adaptability, but because this architecture was reminiscent of another conquering power (the Mughals) with which the British could identify.

PWD engineers inherited the freedom to operate in a non competitive and largely uncritical environment. Their basic designs and infrastructure were meant to supplement any kind of superimposed model However, there were other constraints. First, the Department consisted of three clear engineering disciplines, military, civil and mechanical. Each of these professional cadres projected their own ideas and designs and were inevitably in conflict with each other. Army engineers were the backbone of the PWD to begin with, so they jealously guarded that privilege until, after the growth of the Department in 1866, and the advent of newer technologies, more Civil engineers needed to be employed. The differences in thinking between the groups produced bureaucratic tensions and were therefore counterproductive in many ways. This inherent lack of trust in its own functionaries was sufficiently overt for the the Secretary for Public Works in the India Office in 1870 to openly criticise the Government in the following words:

"Governments in general and the Indian Government in particular, behave as if they believed all their servants to be knaves, only to be kept from picking and stealing by being sharply and suspiciously watched. In constituting the Indian Public Works Department the aim seems to have been less to stimulate than to control activity."

Critics of the PWD felt that the Department "had too soon become an over-centralised bureaucracy with all the faults of that deplorable system–wittily defined by one of its victims as Government by files and despatch boxes, tempered by occasional loss of keys."[6] Clearly the Department did not empower or encourage individual enterprise or initiative. The *Bombay Builder* (1860) openly questioned the artistic and creative architectural capabilities of PWD engineers. "How is it that the Architectural Executive Engineer does not know how to turn a pointed arch" it claimed, and alleged that the Department was guilty of using the wrong kind of materials.

Another of the Government's institutionalised agencies was the Archaeological Survey of India. Since its inception in 1862 it was mandated to analyse elements of Indian architecture "scientifically" as opposed to the designs of Indian patrons and builders who had been building for centuries, and to "conserve" the remnants of what the British believed to be "original stone texts" originating from Graeco Roman sources. Between the PWD and the ASI the Government were able to clarify their own thinking on a number of conflicting issues such as these, not excluding the appropriateness of an architectural style to suit Britain's evolving Imperial criteria.

To say the least, the problems confronting these two institutionalised agencies of British India were formidable. Except for a few outstanding examples like the Padmanabhapuram Palace in the erstwhile state of Travancore-Cochin (now Kerala), constructed wholly in wood much of India's secular architecture over the centuries was lost precisely because they were made of wood. Stone and sometimes brick was used in constructing step wells and sunken baths. Some of these like the one in Mohenjo Daro were for community use. Others like the Queen's step well at Patan with its stunning sculpture galleries and/or the royal complex of Adalaj with its many terraces and carved ornamental niches or the architecture of the Rajput princes, survived, and became, with Mughal architecture, one of the principal sources of inspiration for the Indo Saracenics. India's ancient universities like Taxila and Nalanda were also made of brick and stone while the Rajput forts with their exquisite sculptures and ornamentation in stone were certainly not of Graeco

Roman origin. Mughal architecture went into rapid decline after Aurangzeb but its influence spread far south into the Deccan and Maratha kingdoms. The Vijaynagar and Malabar kingdoms by and large retained their own independent styles of architecture and so did the Eastern kingdoms of Tripura, Manipur and Assam.Obviously, much needed to be swallowed and digested by the PWD engineers.

The innovators of the Indo Saracenic tradition narrowed their focus to Islamic motifs because this was the political diktat. They were happy to do so and concentrated on the innovative engineering aspects of these buildings as prototypes of modern architecture. As engineering solutions, they were simple copies of traditional models, free of the inherent contradictions of architectural programmes. However the unavoidable symbolic content of even such simple utilitarian forms and their frequent ornamentation has been the subject of much controversy in recent times. The facade of the Buland Darwaza was faithfully copied complete with crenellations and studded with rhetorical ornamentation before being recreated as the Victoria Memorial in Madras. So also were the cast iron pillars from Glasgow and the tinted glass from Belgium which replaced many of the old columns and wooden pillars of the Amba Vilas Palace in Mysore. There were many others. In fact these buildings represented a vocabulary of forms which represented for European architects the brave new world of science and technology. They also provided employment for a pan Indian workforce of skilled artisans and crafts persons. Some of the creations were handsome, others were pure fantasy and still others, a chaotic jumble of designs, because of their reliance on simulated and often incongruous ornamentation. These contradictions between image and substance led to criticisms about the movement's viability and purpose.

As to the aesthetic value of Indo Saracenic buildings, it is perhaps well accepted that beauty and ugliness do not necessarily match up with what people like or dislike. In fact recent surveys have shown that 39% of people said they liked at least one building they had rated as beautiful while 21% claimed to have disliked at least one building which they earlier thought was quite beautiful.[7] One reason could be that "beautiful" is not the only positive aesthetic judgement. Another explanation is that "beauty" to many people is a standard or benchmark of sorts. What matters more to an architect, especially where public spaces are at issue, is that a building enhances the lives of people who live and work in it.

Unfortunately, this does not seem to have been the case in many Indian cities, including Madras (Chennai). The oldest recorded Indo Saracenic structure in that city, the Chepauk Palace, a part of which collapsed in 2007 and another portion in 2013, is proof enough of the wanton neglect and in some cases, demolition of many of these buildings. The Chepauk complex on 113 acres of land used to house a number of government departments and consisted of two structures, the Humayun Mahal and the Khalas Mahal. According to a report in the Times of India, most of Humayun Mahal has been locked up and "only a few rooms are used by the State Commission for Women and the Department of Industries."[8] Furniture, files, two wheelers and garbage are dumped in the locked portions of the palace. The brick walls are covered with posters and plants grow from many walls. An open sewer runs round the base of the structure.and the old floors bear huge scratch marks. Some of Henry Irwin's own creations like the old cricket pavilion he designed for the Madras Cricket Club and the building to house the offices and showroom of Messrs P.Orr and Sons have been pulled down. The Connemara Library, also designed by him, has been partially restored, although public access is denied, while another of Irwin's well known architectural contributions to the city, namely, the headquarters of the Victoria Technical Institute with its imposing replica of Akbar's Buland Darwaza, is badly in need of restoration. Likewise Chennai's Post and Telegraph building designed by Irwin's predecesor, Chisholm, and is more Travancore than Indo Saracenic, lost its steep roofs which were similar to the end pavilions.There are others.

In her book Stories of Empire, Jan Morris sums up Indo Saracenic buildings as "rather dowdy, uncertain buildings on the whole." Her concluding observations are relevant.

"British architecture in India," says Morris, *"is anything but avant garde . . . the genre, like the Empire that gave it birth, went out gently, even apologetically in the end . . . (it was) the sort of architecture (that) well suited the needs and preferences of officials and businessmen alike, and could easily be touched up with ornamental elephants or even corner kiosks to show willing to the indigenes. It was hardly architecture at all, really."*[9]

Notes

1. Peter Scriver ed and Vikramaditya Prakash (Colonial Modernities (Routledge London and New York 2007)
2. Ibid
3. Ibid
4. Ibid
5. Paul Walker: Institutional Audiences and Architectural Style in Peter Scriver ed. Colonial Modernities (Routledge 2007)
6. Op cit.
7. Julian Baggini: Report of the Commission for Architecture and the Built Environment's People and Places Project. April 2013
8. Times of India, Sept. 23, 2013
9. Jan Morris: Stones of Empire (Oxford University Press 2005)

CHAPTER 9

CULTURAL COMMITMENT OR MISPLACED PRIORITIES

The Indo Saracenic movement spanned mostly Western and Southern India. It was virtually unknown in Eastern India for several reasons. After the defeat of Nawab Siraj-ud-Daulah at Plassey, 1757, and the decline of Murshidabad as the capital of Bengal, Calcutta became an area more or less exclusive to the colonisers to establish credibility and ultimately moral superiority, over an indigenous population. As the capital of Bengal and later, of the whole of British India, the British quietly and imperceptibly eliminated all competition from native architecture. Calcutta was an extension of the Sunderbans and all that was needed to defend it from invading Nawabi armies and other marauders like the Maratha "bargis" was to move the local inhabitants out of the southern village of Govindapur and build a new impregnable fort on the banks of the Hooghly. The city itself was divided into two clear enclaves–the Black and White towns. The locals lived in the Black town and the Colonials in the White town. The difference between the two was stark. Beyond superficialities, there was no active engagement with the local culture or its people. The new rulers had the freedom to build monuments, churches and public buildings in their own image. The stylistic elements of European neo classicism were deliberately paraded before a captive audience to eclipse existing religious and aesthetic issues. Ian Baucom in his study of "Englishness" quotes Homi K. Bhabha Professor of English at Harvard who refers to the attempts by administrators of Empire "to secure the boundaries of their own identities in order to discipline the identitities of their subjects."[1] Much earlier, in 1873, T. Roger Smith addressing the Royal Society of Arts described Imperial architecture as "a rallying point both for the auto disciplining of the European colonists "and for creating an auratic site before which the native would submit with respect to the reformation of his or her identity."[2] While in the early years of British occupation, there was a weak attempt to imitate elements of Mughal architecture, to ensure "continuity" the trend soon withered in favour of buildings imitative of Classical Europe symbolising power and Christian "benevolence." For visitors, the white high steepled churches and collonnaded buildings in the middle of what was essentially a swamp, were spectacular and served as direct links to Empire.

The Hindu style of architecture was never very popular with the Indo Saracenics. It was rejected by the British as being more suitable for temples and not useful for public structures. From another British perspective, it was a style employed by a people who were conquered twice over and therefore not worthy of emulation. However, there were other issues. In Eastern India, several European communities like the Armenians, the Portuguese and the Greeks were in active trading competition with the British. Therefore, the question of setting an image of undiluted British cultural superiority was important. In the North Eastern states of Assam, Tripura and Manipur, architectural styles retained a large degree of autonomy and both temple and palace architecture were strongly influenced by local traditions. This was also true of the architectural and religious heritage of Orissa and neighbouring Bihar. In 18th and 19th century Bengal, the two most important communities were the Bengali zamindars employed by the British as agents or baniyas and the Marwaris, originally moneylenders, who later became traders, property owners, developers and industrialists. Both communities admired and supported–even if superficially–the process of the region's "Westernisation". The Bengali zamindars, rich with their share of the plunder of Bengal initiated by the colonisers, moved into palatial residential buildings in North Calcutta modelled on Europen neo Classical styles overlooking the Black Town while the Marwaris moved south from Burrabazar gradually to mingle with and acquire properties in the White Town. Anglicisation and European rationality were the watchwords. The Indo Saracenic movement, a style of architecture combining Islamic ornamentation with European classical severity, was, at best pseudo. It was unlikely to appeal to a burgeoning urban Indian audience impatient to rid itself of the Mughal yoke. The indigenous non Islamic architecture of Bengal lacked a theoretical architectural base, to call its own. On the contrary, British Revival styles of the period, be it Renaissance or Jacobethan or Edwardian, served the twin function of association and sensual effect. It is ironic that following the decline of Mughal supremacy in this part of the country, even the palace of the erstwhile Nawab of Murshidabad was redesigned and built by an Englishman in the Palladian style while Prince Gholam Mohammed Shah, 11th son of Tipu Sultan, serving out his sentence of exile in Calcutta thought it best to change loyalties in mid stream and to adopt European manners and customs, including, among other things, European architectural styles and motifs for his mosques and civic buildings.

Madras (Chennai) is considered to be the starting point of the Indo Saracenic movement. In 1768 following the Carnatic wars between the English and French, which ended with the English victory over their rivals, Paul Benfield a Company Engineer in the service of the Nawab of Arcot was called upon by that gentleman to design and build Chepauk palace, near Fort St George in that city. Displaying distinctly Indian overtones, the Palace was completed with typical Islamic domes minarets and pointed arches and remained as a royal residence until 1856. The English acceded to this unusual request because the Nawab was under their protection and Paul Benfield had earlier built the fortifications of the British citadel. Besides a celebration of an Indo British *entente*, the move culminated in the British Government taking over the Nawab's debts in 1801 which were not inconsiderable and the subsequent acquisition by the British of the Carnatic, the name given to the stretch of India's coastline from Ganjam District in Orissa down to Cape Comorin at the southern tip of the Peninsula.

One might well ask why the British did not also settle for an Italianate or neo classical European style of architecture for their public buildings in Madras. A possible explanation is that unlike Bengal, the East India Company's principal rivals in South India at the time were the French, not the Mughals or their vassals. It suited the Company's policy to woo the Muslim rulers of the South against Hindu Maratha rulers like Chanda Sahib who was backed by the French. The *entente*, as we have seen, only lasted a few years and in 1855 the Government decided to abolish the title of Nawab of the Carnatic and pension the next heir to it. However the Nawabs remained loyal to the British. Subsequently, the palace at Chepauk was sold off by public auction and became the offices of the Board of Revenue and the Headquarters of the PWD. Although as Paul Walker observes, the use of an architecture arguably of Mughal origins was of "doubtful pertinence to the local Tamil population",[3] successive Governors of Madras like William Denison and Lord Napier continued to pursue the idea that the presidency town of Madras, like its counterparts in Calcutta and Bombay "had an importance and role in serving and representing British India that went well beyond its immediate territory and population." Napier, in particular, was critical of conventional English styles. He was in favour of incorporating Byzantine elements, a reconciliation between Europe and Asia, distinct from the rest of Indian architecture and yet in keeping with "one capital section of the ancient monuments of the country."[4] The Indo Saracenic style seemed best fitted to match this description.

In 1876, James Fergusson launched a scathing attack on Indian architecture in general and the architecture of the ancient Tamils in particular. Between 1835 and 1842, Fergusson travelled extensively all over India, documenting, as scrupulously as he could, the evolution of Indian architecture. Although his views were contested by later scholars like Vincent Smith, E.B. Havell and Hermann Goetz they were all agreed on the basics, ie., that Indian architecture had evolved from Graeco Roman sources, that it was stagnating and that it was necessary to "preserve" and "improve" Indian architecture.[5] Fergusson had already drawn an outline of Indian architectural history by dividing it into religious and racial characteristics, eg. Aryan/Dravidian and Sanskritic/ non Sanskritic cultures. He conferred a mediocre intellectual status on the South Indians and felt that South Indian civil architecture, or what was left of it, was in an even greater state of decline than in the north. These sentiments were echoed by Smith and others and consciously influenced the introduction of a hybrid style like the Indo Saracenic as being appropriate to a "waning empire" and also to counter criticisms of "poverty of design and detail" in the utilitarian architecture of the Public Works Department of British India.[6]

The Indo Saracenic movement gained official recognition as late as 1890 when Swinton Jacob another engineer turned architect in the service of the State of Jaipur published his well known *Jeypore Portfolio* in twelve volumes, containing drawings of some 600 buildings built in India across several centuries. However, as we have already seen, the movement had started and taken roots well before then. Besides the work of Chisholm, Irwin and others, the revival of the arts and crafts movement in England found a receptive home and official recognition of the skill of Indian craftspersons in the *Journal of Indian Art and Industry* (1883) a lavishly illustrated and meticulously produced account of the work of Indian craftsmen in a variety of fields from enamel and textiles to mosaic design. Ironically, this movement, was a kind of reaction to the technical advances of the Industrial Revolution in England which were of little interest to professional architects intent on recreating the achievements of other ages and civilisations.

Jacob's Department was responsible for everything in the state of Jaipur ranging from outhouses, guardhouses, roads, canals and public buildings. However, Jaipur had a pre British, Rajput history and while commissioning Jacob to design railway and engineering works including some public monuments like the Albert Hall Museum, Maharajah Sawai Jai

Singh was careful to entrust cenotaphs, residences and temples intended for his private use to local artisans/craftsmen paid out of his privy purse. Only Mubarrak Mahal which was meant as a reception hall for entertaining visiting British officials, was permitted to be built in the British colonial/Indo Saracenic style.

The reactions of the rulers of the other Indian princely states to the new colonial style of architecture are equally interesting. The Maharaja of Kapurthala, for example, had a French chateau built by French architects in the heart of the Punjab, while others like the Maharajas of Gwalior and Indore preferred the European classical or neo Italianate styles for their territories. The Maharajas of Kota and Bikaner opted for the Indo Saracenic style. In general, the reluctance by these royals to accept the Indo Saracenic code was prompted by the princes' claim to be "modern" and on an "equal status" with the rulers. In the swing of political loyalties, and in the hope of gaining the confidence and acceptance by their colonial masters, the Palladian palace, rightly or wrongly, appealed to the rulers' taste and presented a more favourable option. Nowhere was this trend more in evidence than in the British government's decision to build a school for the education of the sons of the Rajput Princes at Ajmer. When consulted over their choice of a style, the Princes opted for a European classical style. However the British proceeded on their own steam, to put up an Indo Saracenic building, arguing that this represented the Rajput tradition and hence more appropriate for an institution in which their sons were to be educated! This philosophy of giving back to India what was rightly hers, was based on the presumption that the colonial ruler could educate the Indian about his own heritage.

Two other factors were destined to halt the Indo Saracenic movement in its tracks. First, despite British protestations to the contrary, the involvement of Indian raw material, skills and craftsmanship was limited to executing projects directly under the surveillance of European architects/engineers. This restricted creativity and artistic independence. A good example can be provided by the carvings and entrance gateways to decorate the Jaipur Hall of the Imperial and Colonial exhibition of 1886. Swinton Jacob created the design, the wood was exported from Bombay and the workmen were instructed to freely carve patterns which were "purely Indian." In the rationale of the thinking prevalent at the time, British engineers like Swinton Jacob even thought of "disassembling" elements of Indian architecture to evolve the new style. Reviewing the creations by the Jat Rajas of Deeg, General Cunningham of the Archaeological Survey of India is said to have observed that they were "purely Mohomedan" in style with "very little trace of the real Hindu architecture about it either in its outlines or in its details."[7] According to Cunningham the plain hemispherical or round dome was as Islamic as it was Hindu. These observations were doubtless reflected in Henry Irwin's creations in South India and his association with Indian colleagues in that part of the country.

The second and more important consideration was the firm and conclusive decision by Lord Curzon (Viceroy of India from 1898-1905) that nothing short of a European classical style could possibly convey the spirit of British Imperialism to commemorate Queen Victoria's reign as Empress of India. Curzon, a product of Eton and Oxford, was convinced that the liberalism of his predecessors like Ripon needed to be corrected. While he was not inclined to side with the segment of Indian society which demanded equal rights regardless of skin colour, he did not also believe in apartheid. Curzon was the kind of aristocrat whose aim was to transfer the hierarchical structure inherent in British society to Britain's Indian subjects at all levels. He was, to borrow the term used by Niall Fergusson, a Tory-entalist.[8] Curzon had an appetite for grand architecture (it was during his time that the Taj Mahal and Fatehpur Sikri were restored and the Victoria Memorial was built in Calcutta). He also courted the aristocratic rural landowners of India and the rulers of the princely states as long as they declared their unconditional loyalty to the crown. In the matter of architecture, especially in the building of Calcutta's Victoria Memorial, his letter to Queen Victoria is relevant. "What I shall want", he wrote, "is a simple severe, but noble Italianate building."[9] Looking at the dome, the collonaded porticoes and the doors and windows of the monument which has now become a symbol of this colonial city, the influence of Christopher Wren is unmistakeable. It was not, as many people have been led to believe, a "poor copy" of the Taj. Earlier, the Viceroy's residence in Calcutta was modelled on the Curzon family home in Kedleston, England, by the Marquis of Wellesley.

The Indo Saracenics tried to lay claim on the architecture of New Delhi as the logical extension of a movement that started almost a century ago. However this view was shortsighted if not incorrect. Lutyens' evaluation of the Indo Saracenic style imposed as it was from above without the emotion and ethos that surrounded the originals, was not very flattering. He described the "towers and domes" of Madras as the Raj's own "particular form of vulgarity."[10] He was equally critical of other Indo Saracenic buildings such as Jaipur's Albert Hall or the Daly College in Indore not to mention some of the monstrosities in Bombay which have passed the test of time and the Indo Saracenic stamp. Lutyens was primarily a classicist and an aesthete, an architect with a vision who believed that the best of India's architecture could be incorporated into beaux arts classicism to express modern India in stone without sacrificing the ideals of Imperialism. He hoped that his creations would one day become a new and inspiring period in the history of Indian art. Later evaluations of Lutyens' stunning creativity have confirmed that this was indeed the case.

In the ultimate analysis, there were major differences between the Revivalist movement in Britain and its colonies. In England and elsewhere in Europe, notwithstanding the confrontations that happened at many levels–religion, politics, science, education and the arts–there was a historical continuity. The age of Baroque with its splendid buildings gave way to delicacy, restraint and refinement while the arts of Egypt, India and the Far East offered exotic delights as well as serious instruction. The English Revival style of architecture was popular around the 1830s and derived most of its inspiration from the Italian Renaissance (1450-1535). Queen Anne architecture, often described as romantic and feminine was probably a by-product of the Industrial Revolution but ran counter to it in many ways. The neo Renaissance style of Charles Barry (architect of the London Houses of Parliament) incorporated many elements from the Perpendicular Gothic of A.W.N. Pugin and the Romanesque style. Pugin, a purist in matters Gothic, believed that "every building that is treated naturally, without disguise or concealment, cannot fail to look well."[11] Neo classical and Palladian styles introduced by architects like George Dance, Henry Holland, John Soanes and others were pressed into service to provide a whole new series of designs borrowed from Italian and French prototypes initiated in a previous period by the Adam brothers, John Nash and Christopher Wren. All of the above movements were based on written texts, the connections between architecture and society of the time, and the integrity of patrons and architects, not to mention the exclusive significance of ornamentation and embellishments.

Victorian and Edwardian India's architectural scenario, by contrast, was quite different, as were the principal issues. The main consideration of the colonisers, as will have been evident from previous chapters, was to project British Imperialism and sovereignty in a variety of ways. Architecture, preferably of an exotic variety, was a by-product of this thinking. However, the British did not bargain for the "impenetrability" of Indian homes and the Indian psyche. They therefore confined their attentions to royal palaces and public spaces. Even here they bypassed cultural considerations and spatial arrangements– for example, the physical measures taken by Indian rulers to transform their courts into fortified citadels, the relationships between spaces in these complexes designated for formal receptions, religious functions, accommodation for kings, courtiers and female members of the royal family and so on. One of the hypotheses on which the "continuity" theory of the Indo Saracenic movement was based was that by enhancing the physical configuration of the built environment, as in places like Lahore and other smaller towns in India, social and moral improvement was possible. Lahore was once a splendid Mughal city which remained derelict for many years until it was made the provincial capital of the Punjab in the early 20th century. Here the process of "Indianization" was turned upside down. As with many north Indian cities, Lahore's Imperial buildings were used as government offices and barracks for British troops. The Governor's official residence (Government House) was built around the tomb of a Mughal nobleman, Qasim Khan Mir Bahr. Likewise, the Residency, which housed the Lawrence family was built around another Mughal tomb– the tomb of the legendary Anarkali. Lahore's Moti Masjid was converted to a treasury while nearby Aurangzeb's great Badshahi Masjid continued to be used as a magazine.

Prof.Mark Crinson of the University of Manchester in the Introduction to one of his books makes the point that "at two extremes it (colonial architecture) either stands for the rapacity and racial self delusion of Empire or for a world of lost glory and forgotten convictions." A third reaction, perhaps less political than these, simply finds nothing but absurdity in these images, such as "a Lincolnshire church in the hot dusty maidan of a tropical city"[12] or of an Italianate front to a coventional PWD type structure in an Art Gallery in South India. Not without reason he asks if Englishness was imposed on these societies. Clearly, Indo Saracenic architecture was an attempt to test Victorian "eclectic" theories to help forge elements of a new ideology.The idea was, at best, immature and unrealistic. The historical origins of the movement and the rhetoric of cultural commitment were also doubtful. Predictably, therefore, it was overtaken by circumstances, its own inconsistencies and inherent contradictions.

Notes

1. Ian Baucom: Englishness, Empire and the Locations of Identity (Princeton, 1999)
2. T. Roger Smith: Architecture and Representation of Empire in India (1860-1910)
3. Paul Walker: Institutional Audiences and Architectural Style (Essay in Colonial Modernities ed Peter Scriver & Vikramaditya Prakash, Routedge, 2007)
4. Peter Scriver and Vikramaditya Prakash ed. Colonial Modernities (Routledge 2007)
5. Ibid
6. Ibid

7. Ibid

8. Niall Fergusson: Empire (Allen Lane and Penguin 2003/2004)

9. Ibid

10. T. Metcalf: An Imperial Vision (London, Faber 1989)

11. The Modern World, ed. Norbert Lynton London (Paul Hamlyn 1965)

12. Mark Crinson: Empire Building, Orientalism and Victorian Architecture (Routledge 1986)

CHAPTER 10

EPILOGUE

Like the fantasy that was Indo Saracenic architecture, its own unrealistic base–British India's penchant for ornamentalism, pomp and pageantry–was also rapidly falling apart. The paradigm of hierarchy and social inequality which David Cannadine argues was "the vehicle for the extension of British social structures to the ends of the world" was, of course, employed in India to justify the apparent similarities between the two cultures, with one difference. The cult of hierarchy was an oversimplification of something infinitely more complex,[1] Second, the misplaced British faith in comparatives with the mother country was to generate and perpetuate a devolution of power through greater or lesser chiefs at levels far removed from Westminster or Whitehall. This was regressive. Both British and Indian social traditions had their separate identities and functioned under different compulsions. Third, the role of race in the whole drama of Empire can hardly be overlooked or bypassed. Brtish Imperialists looked down on the average Indian or African as much as they did on their own lower orders.Until well into the 19th century, the Empire flourished on the basis of military conquests and dictatorship, martial law and "special "courts, extermination and genocide. The future King Edward VII's remarks about King Kalakua of Hawaii to which I referred earlier is, of course, relevant.

After the Uprising of 1857 and the official proclamation of Empire the following year, it was increasingly apparent that the true foundations of British power in India were not the Maharajas or their elephants but the elite of Anglicised lawyers and civil servants Macaulay had called into existence.[2] Indeed as the 20th Century dawned, Colonial rule displayed signals that it had begun to survive in India largely by default and was about to end soon. Even as Churchill from his ivory tower in the House of Commons thundered that British policy towards India was a "hideous act of self mutilation" and deplored the "liberal" policy of his Tory associates, things were changing. Earlier, Lord Dufferin, addressing a gathering at Calcutta on the eve of his retirement from the Viceroyalty of India, referred to the leaders of the Indian National Congress as "a microscopic minority incapable of self government" while the Ilbert Bill passed in 1883 had led to a virtual white revolution within the Government. Ironically, English educated middle and upper class Indians within its ranks, loyal to the Empire did not conceive of or even desire, the termination of English rule. Men like Dadabhai Naoroji petitioned only for a degree of equality and self representation. However, all this did not reflect reality.

First, in the two decades after 1920 the country witnessed an unprecedented population growth, from 306 million in 1921 to 400 million in 1947. Notwithstanding the large influx of gold from the sub continent, Britain's financial interests in India were also declining. The country was manufacturing its own cotton goods and Indian business had begun to develop independently of the British. Threatened with resignations from the Viceroy's Executive Council, Britain could neither impose protective tariffs on English textiles as in the past nor persuade the Government from paying for requipment of the Indian Army before the Second World War. The induction and promotion of Indian officers both in the Army and Civil Services led to a further erosion of power while the supply of indentured labour on which the British Imperial economy depended also declined sharply towards the end of the 19th century. Indeed the growth of British per capita gross domestic by 347%, against the Indian comparative, of a mere 14% in 200 years of British rule, admirably fitted Nehru's description of the state of the alien Government in India as a tooth still strongly embedded but in an advanced state of decay.[3] Clearly, India was a "declining asset". The rest of India's freedom struggle, leading to the events of 1947 are only too well known and do not bear repetition.

Like all revolutions, Indian nationalism was fuelled not by the impoverishment of the many but by the rejection of the privileged few. The result, as Niall Fergusson observes was that by the end of Queen Victoria's term as Empress of India, British rule was like one of those palaces Curzon so adored. It looked simply splendid on the outside. But downstairs the servants were busy turning the floorboards into firewood.[4] In 1897 Rudyard Kipling wrote these prophetic lines:

> *Far called our navies melt away*
> *On dune and headland sinks the fire:*
> *Lo, all our pomp of yesterday*
> *Is one with Nineveh and Tyre!*
> *Judge of the nations, spare us yet, Lest we forget–lest we forget!*

Following the Amritsar massacres of 1919, the Khilafat Movement of the 1920s, Gandhi's promises of "Purna Swaraj" the Civil Disobedience Movement of the '30s and the impact of the Second World War, British India had become decidedly shaky and willing to negotiate the terms of self government. If the first World War over extended the Empire, commented Richard Gott in "The Guardian" the Second World War which in the end turned out to be a war against racism accelerated its downfall. If it was right to oppose Hitler it was as necessary to dismantle an Empire built on the same racial principles as the Nazi Reich. Curzon who was possibly the last Viceroy to try and maintain Imperialist rule by "modernizing" it to include a reliable aristocracy of "listed" Indian elite, was bypassed by his own Tory leadership in England "as representing that section of privileged conservatism" which no longer had a place "in this democratic age."[5]

In August 1947, after the tumult and the shouting, when the last British troops marched out of the Gateway of India the curtain came down on an era which in some quarters still evokes nostalgic memories. The Empire had ended in the immortal words of T.S. Eliot, "not with a bang but with a whimper."[6] Alas, Macaulay's ghost continues to haunt the minds of the so called elite of this country, and it is for consideration if the mythical veil of the "white man's burden" will ever be lifted. To quote the poet again, "That corpse you planted last year in your garden, Has it begun to sprout? Will it bloom again this year? Or has the sudden frost disturbed its bed?"[7] One wonders . . .

Notes

1. David Cannadine: How the British Saw Their Empire: London, (Allen Lane 2001)
2. Niall Fergusson: Empire London (Penguin 2003)
3. Ibid
4. Richard Gott: The Guardian, London, May 5, 2001
5. Niall Fergusson: Op. cit.
6. T.S. Eliot: The Hollow Men (London 1925)
7. T.S. Eliot: The Wasteland and Other Poems (London 1922)

APPENDIX 1

HENRY IRWIN: 1841-1922

1864 Entry into the Office Survey of Coastguard buildings Department of Public Works, The Admiralty as Member of the Institute of Civil Engineers

1866 Public Works Dept. PWD (Ceylon)

1868 Public Works Department, India

1871 Marriage to Henrietta Helen nee Irwin, in Ireland

1872 Executive Engineer, Nagpur and Central Provinces

1872-1881 Designs and builds the Christ Church at Panchmarhi

1881 Move to Simla as Superintendent of Works Imperial Circle

1881-1888 Designed and built many public buildings including the new Viceregal Lodge on Observatory Hill

1886 Civil Engineer

1888 Superintending Engineer and Secretary Public Works to Rajputana and Central Provinces

1888 New Viceregal Lodge, Simla inaugurated by Lord Dufferin

1888 Awarded the CIE

1888 Appointed Consulting Architect to the Govt. of Madras.

1888-1896 Designs and builds several monuments in the city in the Indo Saracenic style some of which were completed after his death

1896 Retires to Mount Abu in Rajputana (Rajasthan)

1897 Receives contract to design a new palace in Mysore to replace the one destroyed by fire the previous year

1922 Henry Irwin moves to Loch End, Ootacamund

1922 (5th August) Henry Irwin dies at Ooty.

NB Between 1871 and 1884 Irwin's wife, Henrietta, gave birth to six daughters and four sons, one of whom died, prematurely in Simla. All of his children were born in Nagpur/Panchmarhi and/or Simla.

APPENDIX 2A

BRITISH ARCHITECTURE FROM 1550 ONWARDS

The differences between European classical architecture and the Indo Saracenic style are striking. The former by and large corresponds to the principles laid down by the ancient Roman architect, Vitruvius which are (a) function (b) structure and (c) beauty. In the study of these buildings, it is usual, therefore, to look for elements of design, compatibility with the environment, their structures and ability to age well and, not least, their appeal to our sense of proportion and balance. Partisans of the latter were more concerned with what was fashionable and politically appropriate. By the mid 19th century a particular kind of architectural orientalism had emerged in Britain. This could be seen in a variety of forms: in the writings of architects like Owen Jones and John Ruskin, as well as in the popular content of The Great Exhibition of 1851 which, among other things, sought to make clear to the world that Britain was the indisputable industrial leader of the world. A number of neo Islamic buildings were built in England during this period. They were modelled on Islamic monuments in the Middle East but later described by Edward Said and others as being based on insufficient knowledge about the East and from pre conceived archetypes.

The Indo Saracenic style was an obvious offshoot of this movement. By contrast to the European Neo Classical and Gothic Revival styles which were current in Europe and India before the advent of this particular brand, the Indo Saracenic style was seen as pseudo, hybrid and ambiguous in its design and execution. Some called the concept eclectic, others described it as pure fantasy. A few of the buildings, like the old museum in Mathura designed and executed by Indian craftsmen under the supervision of an ICS officer, F.S. Growse were quite beautiful, others frankly outlandish, like the Muir College in Allahabad designed by the well known architect, William Emerson. However there was no doubting the crusading and purposeful intentions of the movement.

As a matter of fact, the 18th and 19th centuries witnessed a period of architectural exhuberance in England. The multiplicity of styles presented the designer with unprecedented opportunities. The Palladian style initiated by Andrea Palladio in Italy, dominated British architecture until mid 18th century as a reaction to Baroque ornamentalism. Palladian buildings consisted of clearly defined spaces designed on a strict system of proportions and externally, sparingly decorated. Facades were marked by triangular pediments and straight lines above a rusticated plinth level. The new aesthetic theory considered buildings not as independent self contained formal units but as component parts of their environment. In England, this was the English landscape garden, popularised by persons like Alexander Pope, William Kent and Lancelot (alias Capability) Brown. It is interesting how these and similar concepts were transported to India through the paintings of William Hodges, the uncle and nephew team of Thomas and William Daniell and others.

Between the middle and late eighteenth centuries, the Palladian style gave way to neo Classicism associated with such names as James Stuart (alias Athenian Stuart) because of his interest in Greek antiquities, Nicholas Revett and later Robert Adam (1728-1792) also known as the father of of the British Neo Classical movement. In fact Kedleston Hall, which was copied by the Marquis of Wellesley to serve as the Viceroy's official residence in Calcutta, was designed by Adam. This elegant style, seen in such creations as Syon House, Kenwood House and the building of the Royal Society of Arts in London, the Adelphy, also found their way to the sub continent. The style fell out of fashion in 1770s and although it was perpetuated by John Wood and his son in the Circus and Royal Crescent in Bath it was overtaken by a return to the Gothic Revival featuring names like Sir Christopher Wren, John Vanbrugh and Horace Walpole. Still later, the independent Neo Classical designs of Sir John

Soane with elements of Greek antiquity and the equally striking architecture of John Nash characterised by collonades, porticoes and palatial edifices swept through London and the British Isles.

In England, neo classicism was the first choice in the secular or civic architecture of the period but there was a complex of interrelated developments. British national pride expressed itself in reviving the architecture of Elizabethan (Tudor) with Jacobean (Stuart) styles. There were other elements. As a result of the influence of the Orientalists, The Royal Pavilion at Brighton, basically a Georgian building was transformed by John Nash into a pleasure palace compounded of Indian Gothic and Chinese elements. On the other hand, the rationality and moralistic values of the Anglican (High Church) movement of England adopted Perpendicular Gothic as their medium of expression. All of these ideas were exported to and implemented in, the British colonies in varying degrees of authenticity and purpose.

Into this world of Tuscan villas, classical town houses and Gothic castles came the engineering innovations of the Industrial Revolution. While these figured prominently on the credit side of the Industrial balance sheet of the time, they cast a shadow on the genteel and protected realm of architecture and came increasingly to be associated with museums, railway stations and sewage plants. The principle of what came to be known as the "picturesque" was replaced on the one hand by a variety of unreal environments–quite a bit of which was inspired by the architecture of the Orient–and on the other, by Pugin's moralistic views by which he made strict demands on the integrity of patrons and architects and even pointed out some of the flaws of advanced Victorian thought arguing that "only admiration worth having attached itself wholly to the meaning of sculpture and colour on the building . . . what we call architecture is only the association of these in noble masses, or the placing of them in fit places. All architecture, other than this is, in fact, mere building."[1]

The following pages will serve to illustrate examples of British architecture exported to the Colonies including India, with varying degrees of modification:

1. Elizabethan and Jacobean (Mid 16th-17th Century)

The main features were wings on either side of a central porch like the letter "E" although quadrangles were not unknown. Some Elizabethan mansions were half timbered. They had elaborate fireplaces, grand staircases, strapworks and oak wood panelling. The porch sometimes reaches right upto the roof of the house. Ceilings are covered with plaster and moulded into patterns. The staircse built in straight flights around a square well has taken the place of the Gothic spiral and upstairs, running the whole length of the house there is a very long narrow room called the Long Gallery. Inside and outside are carved moulded patterns.

2. English Renaissance(17ᵗʰ Century)

This period of English architecture is associated with the name of Inigo Jones who studied under the Italian architect, Andrea Palladio. The style is simple and dignified. The buildings are rectangular with no gables, projections or wings. The windows, unlike the previous period are small in proportion to the wall space and arranged at regular intervals. Each window is set in a stone frame and sometimes there is a pediment, either half round or triangular, headed above each. Sometimes, pillasters are placed between the windows along the face of the building. Columns are correct in their proportions and support horizontal lintels. Other features include collonades, arches and the effect known as "rustication", ie., the base of th building is made up of large stone blocks separated from each other by deep grooves. Some 17ᵗʰ century houses had "hipped' roofs, ie., the slope upto a central ridge from all four sides. Others had "dormer" windows, which seemed to grow out of the roof. There is a lot of panelling using moulded plaster and wood. Sir Christopher Wren, who redesigned London's St Paul's Cathedral was very much associated with the English Renaissance style, which also featured the sash window–the quintessential English window, in two parts, each of which could be pushed up or down separately.

3. Queen Anne and Georgian (18th Century)

This century initiated the advent of row houses, collonaded doors with fanlights, canopies and pediments. Fanlights which are a feature of many houses of the period were like glass panels to light the hall and the delicate ribs to hold the glass are often arranged like the spokes of an open fan. Sash windows are either rectangular or rounded and sometimes outside the windows there may be graceful little wrought iron railings. Nearly all windows have an architrave round them. The century also witnessed a refinement of plaster mouldings, wrought iron rails and balustrades. Two brothers, Robert and James Adam were famous architects of the period. They introduced round headed niches for statues, oval plaques and many other decorative features like the classic Greek urn, also known as the Adam Urn. The bow window often used as a shop front, as distinct from the bay window in ealier Jacobethan homes was another striking architectural innovation of the period. Britain celebrated visual effectiveness in its architecture through the work of John Nash and John Soane. The dramatic sweep of London's Regent Street or the Royal Crescent at Bath are outstanding examples of the former's genius as was his work, albeit at a different level, on the Royal Pavilion at Brighton, a basically Georgian building which Nash transformed into a pleasure palace compounded of Indian Gothic and Chinese elements.

4. English Perpendicular Gothic (19th Century)

In the 19th Century the English architect A.W.N. Pugin equated Gothic architecture with "Christian" architecture. The style became popular in India because it fitted English evangelist aspirations of the time and because it was an important statement of national pride intended to evoke a period of religious and civic greatness in the Middle Ages. Its main features were strong vertical lines, large windows with elaborate tracery fan vaulting, hammerbeam roofs and many others. Many important 19th century English civic buildings like the Houses of Parliament and the Law courts were built in this style. Pugin's moralistic views on the rationality of Gothic design and the severity of Christian architecture as an antithesis to the "pagan" or "heathen" implications of Graeco Roman temples were not only supported by the well known art critic, John Ruskin; the style also seemed to lend itself more easily to Orientalisation.

Notes

1. The Modern World ed. Norbert Lynton, London, (Hamlyn 1965)

APPENDIX 2B

EUROPEAN RELIGIOUS ARCHITECTURAL TYPES:

1. GREEK	Tall columns supported by a lintel and pitched roof structure running the length of the building: triangular, heavily decorated gables; Columns Ionic, Doric (no base), Tuscan. Cella or inner sanctum
2. ROMAN	Similar to Greek except for (i) structural arch–the motif of an arch within an entablature frame and (ii) the hemispherical dome.
3. EARLY CHRISTIAN/ BYZANTINE (c4)	5 aisled basilicas, dome, mosaic decoration, outer narthex or porch, Christian motifs on capitals eg acanthus leaves wound round a Christian cross.
4. ROMANESQUE (c10-12)	Round arches, small apsidal chapels, layers of round headed windows, heavy geometric decoration on walls round arches of the nave supported by clusters of pillars, blind arcading, ornamental columns, heavily decorated doors

5. GOTHIC (c12)	Pointed arch higher and lighter than Romanesque, tall towers with spires rib vaults, flying buttresses, elegant ambulatories use of tall mullions and horizontal transoms (Eng. Perpendicular) rich surface treatments
6. RENAISSANCE (c15 onwards)	Pedimented facades, arcades and entablatures, decorative obelisks, multi symmetrical facades, square towers designs based on antique motifs
7. BAROQUE & ROCCOCO (c17 onwards)	Curving facades, joint orders of pillasters, wall surfaces rusticated, curved pediments heavy ornamentation spread over walls ceilings and other surfaces.
8. PALLADIAN (c18)	Pedimented temple fronts sometimes mounted on a podium dormer windows temple fronted rotundas, coffered rotundas
9. NEO-CLASSICAL (c19)	Combination of Greek revival and Renaissance features, uniform porticos of Tuscan columns eg. John Nash Regents Park, London
10. GOTHIC REVIVAL (c19 Eng)	Use of plaster and wood a significant style for churches, tall towers, style associated with attempts to revive the perceived religious fervour of the Middle Ages
11. VICTORIAN (late c19)	Combination of Greek Roman Renaissance Baroque and Queen Anne motifs

THE QUEEN'S HOUSE GREENWICH

HALF TIMBERED ELIZABETHAN HOUSE

A WREN STYLE HOUSE

TYPICAL ENGLISH TOWN HOUSE WITH TRIANGULAR
AND SEMI CIRCULAR PEDIMENTS AND BALCONIES

EARLY 18TH CENTURY PANELLED DOOR
WITH SHELL HOOD

LATE 18TH CENTURY PANELLED DOOR
WITH PILASTERS AND DECORATIVE LINTEL

PANELLED DOOR
WITH TUSCAN PILLARS, FANLIGHT AND
TRIANGULAR PEDIMENT

ENGLISH PARISH CHURCH

A WREN MASTERPIECE:
ST. PAUL'S CATHEDRAL, LONDON

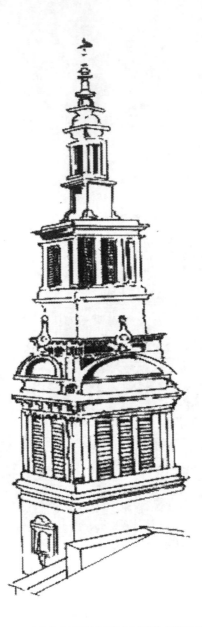

ENGLISH RENAISSANCE
TOWER AND STEEPLE

DORMER WINDOW

GEORGIAN BOW WINDOW

SASH WINDOW

APPENDIX 3

THE MUGHAL ETHOS

Essentially, the Mughal contribution to South Asian architecture were tombs, palaces and mosques. The Mughals ruled India, a largely non Islamic country and if, in the earlier years they ignored the non Islamic elements of Indian architecture, the attitude changed quite substantially from the reign of Akbar (1556-1605) when Hindu elements were incorporated into the Muslim tradition.

Mughal architecture was possibly derived from Central Asian prototypes, the Seljuks and the Timurids to name just two. We have only to look at the multiple storied towers of the 14th century pre Moghul Atala Mosque in Jaunpur with its massive archway and decorative detail which completely obscures the dome behind it, reminding us of the Seljuk ivan hall court mosque in Turkey or the Mausoleum of

Sultan Sher Shah another pre Mughal structure considered to be one of the most important pre Mughal monuments of its type in India. This latter building, built on an octagonal plan consists of two stories surmounted by a dome with terraces and corners decorated with canopied pavilions. The main central dome surrounded by smaller secondary domes are distinctly Timurid in inspiration and the entire structure built in sandstone stands on a granite platform on an island in an artificial lake. Other Timurid influences include interconnecting and stacked transverse arches, mausolea with a central chamber surrounded by smaller chambers as in Humayun's tomb at Sikandra, and the complex geometrical formulae used in Timurid buildings. The presence of water around funerary monuments and the concept of gardens, both symbolic of Paradise, was also a part of Timurid tradition, as were the rich pictorial and iconographic traditions of the monuments built during this period. Yet another Timurid contribution to Mughal architecture was the concept of large congregational prayer halls or Jami Masjids. Pre Mughal architecture can also be seen in and around Delhi, notably in Tughlakabad and of course in many other regions such as in Gujerat, Bengal and the Deccan.

The style of architecture familiar to us today as specifically "Mughal" reached its peak in the reign of Shah Jahan who built the Taj Mahal in memory of his beloved wife Mumtaz Mahal. This particular monument built of white marble inlaid with coloured stones of all kinds in beautiful abstract and floral patterns and four tall minarets at each corner is regarded as being one of the most famous in world architecture. Other examples are the cities of Fatehpur Sikri built by Akbar in 1575 and the Agra Fort built by Shah Jahan almost a century later. The former with a palace complex and buildings represent a magnificent fusion of Hindu and Muslim traditions as does the unquestionable grandeur of its principal gateway, the Buland Darwaza with its impressive row of bell towers and pavilions. Likewise, the Agra Fort combines some of the best of Hindu and Islamic architecture. The fort consists of a wall over a mile long and stands nearly 70 feet above the surrounding terrain from which it is separated by a ditch about 33 feet deep. It contains the palaces of the Mughal Emperors. Both royal cities display some of the characteristic features of Mughal architecture—the elevation of the palace city above the ground on which they were built, exquisite marble grille work on balustrades and screens in combination with richly developed inlay work, as in the tomb of Itmad-ud Daula, Shah Jahan's father in law, not to mention the blend of large bulbous Timurid domes in combination with Hindu type chhatris (pavilions) in Agra's Pearl Mosque.

As far as secular architecture is concerned, Akbar appears to have been heavily influenced by elements he borrowed from Gwalior's Man Mandir Palace built by Raja Man Singh Tomar especially the concept of connected courtyards with galleries and rooms, eaves or Chhajas with animal brackets and some aspects of the mosaic work on the exterior of that palace. These features were subsequently replicated in Fatehpur Sikri and the Delhi Gate of Agra Fort respectively. Indeed, many of them were incorporated into more decentralised versions of Mughal architecture, including regional variants, in subsequent years.

What is perhaps relevant is that Mughal architecture was not based on mere political authority. Many of the monuments they built especially after the 1500s reflect the Moghul penchant for eclectism and syncretism. They represented the cultural and social values cherished by the people who built them. Huge sections of the population, for example had a stake in creating and utilizing Mughal funerary architecture. The cult of Sufism and related monuments to Sufi saints was widespread. As for the gardens of Mughal India, both formal (the Char Bagh) and informal, these too had their special significance. They were oases for spiritual rejuvenation besides providing a facility for strengthening family, friendship and community bonds, The pools and channels of water provided opportunities for self reflection. There were pavilions for royal visitors and common citizens. In the ultimate analysis, Mughal architecture in all its forms was a celebration of the spirit The difference between these monuments and the less imaginative and largely imitative, Indo Saracenic style, is all too clear.

HENRY IRWIN AND THE INDO SARACENIC MOVEMENT RECONSIDERED

GLOSSARY

Amba Vilas Palace: The name of the palace of the ruling family of Mysore in the state of Karnataka rebuilt by Henry Irwin after the old palace, mainly of timber. was burnt down. Amba is another name for the goddess Durga and Vilas means "the abode of . . ."

Amritsar Massacre: (1919) A seminal event in British India when British troops opened fire on an unarmed group who had gathered in Jallianwallabagh to protest the arrest of two leaders. The dead were estimated at between 370 and 1000 persons.

Ayah: Lady's maid, nurse.

Apse: The curved east end of a church.

Baraset: District Headquarters and Magistracy in the state of West Bengal. Warren Hastings, first Governor General of India built an elegant garden house in the town which was later used as the District Magistrate's official residence by successive ICS officers.

Bay window: A group of three windows placed to form one side of a polygon with corners.

Bow window: A curved bay window.

Beaux-Arts: An elaborate late 19th and early 20th century architectural style.

Bhandarkar, D.R: (1875-1950) Eminent Indian archaeologist and epigraphist who worked with the Archaeological Survey of India.

Camden Society: Founded in 1838 to publish historical and literary materials. It merged with the Royal Historical Society in 1897.

Chennai: Capital city of the state of Tamil Nadu, formerly known as Madras.

Chisholm, R.F.: British architect(1840-1915) who pioneered the Indo Saracenic style of architecture in Madras.

Church Commissioners: A body managing the affairs of the historic property assets of the Church of England.

Clapboard: A type of wooden cladding

Corbel/Corbelling: A projecting block or capital supporting an arch or shaft above.

Cornice: A horizontal decorative moulding.

Coromandel Coast: The Eastern coast of the South Indian peninsula bordering the Bay of Bengal. The name is derived from the Tamil Chola Mandalam (The land of the Cholas)

Crennelations: A parapet with alternating high and low sections.

Curzon Lord Nathaniel: Viceroy of India (1898-1905).

Dentils: Small blocks used as a repeating ornament in the bed mould of a cornice

Dhobi: Washerman.

Dormer window: A window projecting from a roof

Dufferin Lady Harriet: Wife of Lord Dufferin remembered for her commitment to the cause of women in India.

Dufferin, Lord Frederic Hamilton Blackwood: Viceroy of India (1884-1888) succeeding Lord Ripon.

Entablature: The whole of the horizontal structure above the capitals in a Classical Order

Fanlight: A semicircular window over a door.

Fergusson James: Scottish architectural historian remembered for his interest in Indian historical architecture and antiquities.

Finial: The decorative knob on top of a gable, post or other upright.

Georgian: The name given to the style of architecture in Britain and other English speaking countries between 1720 and 1820.

Gothic Revival: An architectural movement which began in England in 1740. The style gained popularity in the 19th century, its most committed exponent being A.W.N. Pugin who also designed the British Houses of Parliament.

Guptas: The name of the ruling dynasty in India from approximately 320-550 AD. The high points of the cultural activities of this period are magnificent architecture, sculptures and paintings.

Haider Ali: (1721-1782) Sultan and de facto ruler of the kingdom of Mysore, remembered for his opposition to British colonial forces during the Anglo Mysore Wars and father of Tipu Sultan.

Hastings, Warren: First Governor General of Bengal (1782-1785) Accused of corruption and impeached. Acquitted after a long trial in 1795.

Hipped roof: A roof pitched at the ends as well as the sides.

Jacob, Swinton: British army officer and colonial engineer known for his compilation of Indian architectural designs known as Jacob's Portfolio.

Jacobethan: A combination of Jacobean and Elizabethan architecture in England, 15th and 16th centuries.

Kanauj: Ancient capital of Emperor Harshavardhan, 590-647 AD.

Khansamah: Cook cum butler.

Khilafat Movement: An essentially pan Islamic movement after World War 1 in support of the Ottoman Empire which won the support of Mahatma Gandhi and the Congress.

Khitmutgar: Table waiter.

Lancet window: A tall narrow pointed early Gothic window.

Lintel: A load bearing beam

Loggia: A gallery with an open collonade along one or more sides.

Lutyens Edwin: Leading British architect (1869-1944) sometimes called "the greatest" who along with Herbert Baker designed the Imperial capital in New Delhi including outstanding monuments such as the Viceroy's House (now known as Rashtrapati Bhavan) India Gate and many others. Claimed by the Indo Saracenics as one of their own, he was in fact highly critical of the style, declaring that it was "the Raj's own particular form of vulgarity."

Malabar Coast: The coastal region of south West India. The name is thought to have been derived from the Malayalam word Mala (hill) and Vaaram (range or region). This latter portion was Westernised to "bar"

Mansard roof: Larger version of hipped roof puctuated by dormer windows.

Mauryas: The Mauryan dynasty ruled India from 322-185 BCE one of the largest empires in its time and the largest in the Indian sub continent.

Mohenjo Daro: An archaeological site in the province of Sindh, Pakistan, it was an ancient city built around 2600 BC.

Morris William: (1834-1896) English artist, writer, textile designer and socialist associated with the Pre Raphaelite and Arts and Crafts movement in Britain.

Mughal: Muslim dynasty of Turkic-Mongol origins that ruled over most of Northern India from the early 16th to the mid 18th centuries.

Mumbai: Contemporary name for thr erstwhile metropolis of Bombay.

Mullion: A vertical element dividing a window into sections.

Mysore: Current name Mahisuru in the state of Karnataka in South India.

Napier, Lord: Viceroy of India from February to May 1872.

Nave: The area of a church reserved for lay people.

Neo classical: An architectural style similar to the Palladian produced by the neo classical movement which began in the mid 18th century

Padmanabhapuram: Magnificent wooden palace of the 16ᵗʰ century and home to the Rajas of Travancore (1550-1750) a fine specimen of Kerala's indigenous style of architecture.

Palladian: A European style of architecture which derives its name from the Italian architect, Andrea Palladio.

Panchmarhi: A hill station in Madhya Pradesh, Central India.

Pataliputra: Adjacent to modern day Patna was an ancient city built by the ruler of Magadha, Ajatasatru in 490 BCE

Pediment: The gable (usually triangular or semicircular) above a Classical door or portico

Pendentive: A curved triangular area beteen a round dome and its rectangular base.

Peterhof: Summer residence of British Viceroys until 1888 built in the mock Tudor style, now a hotel.

Pilaster: A flat column form usually attached to a wall.

Portico: Porch extended by a collonade.

Pugin, A.W.N: (1812-1852) English architect author theorist and designer associated with the Roman Catholic and Gothic Revival movements in Britain.

Purlin: A horizontal beam along the length of a roof.

Purna Swaraj: (January 26, 1930) Formal Declaration of Indian Independence.

Queen Anne: The Queen Anne style of architecture refers vaguely to English Baroque and corresponds to the reign of Queen Anne (1702-1714).

Rani Vannivilasa: Wife of Maharaja Chamaraj Wodeyar of Mysore and mother of Maharaja Krishnaraja Wodeyar IV.

Rose window: Circular window found in Gothic churches divided into segments by stone mullions and tracery.

Rustication: Masonry cut so that the centre of each block projects.

Sash window: A window with with vertically (or occasionally horizontally) sliding wooden frames holding the glass panes.

Simla: Now known as Shimla, was the summer retreat of Viceroys and Governor Generals of British India.

Squinch: The filling between a dome and the building below; less sophisticated than a pendentive.

Syce: Horsekeeper or groom.

Thattikonda Namberumal Chetty: South Indian Master builder and close associate of Henry Irwin.

The Ecclesiologist: Journal of Church architecture. The Ecclesiological Society (founded 1845) was earlier known as the Cambridge Camden Society.

Tipu Sultan: Son of Haider Ali and one of the greatest threats to British supremacy in South India until his death in the Battle of Seringapatam, 1799.

Trabeated: A form of construction with vertical posts and horizontal beams.

Tracery: The decorative stone bars in a Gothic window.

Transom: Horizontal bar across a window, also the upper part of a door frame.

Tudor: The period of English history from 1485- 1603.

Turret: Small tower projecting vertically from the wall of a building

Vijaynagar: Capital of the Vijaynagar kings one of the most powerful ruling Hindu dynasties of South India since 1370 located near Hampi, Bellary District of Karnataka.

Windbracer: A diagonal support linking a series of uprights.

Vishnupur: A sub divisional town in West Bengal, Bankura District.

Wodeyar: The ruling family of Mysore, Karnataka state.

SELECT BIBLIOGRAPHY

1. Asher, Catherine B: Architecture of Mughal India (The New Cambridge History of India, ed. Johnson, Bayley & Richards, Cambridge University Press, 1992)

2. Baginni, Julian: Journal of The Commission for Architecture and The Built Environment (People and Places Project, UK., April 2013)

3. Bosdogan, S: Orientalism &Architectural Culture (J.Stor 1986)

4. Brendan, Pierce: The Decline and Fall of the British Empire,(Alfred Knopf, New York, 2008)

5. Bakshi, Randip: The Birth of Indic Architecture University of Victoria, 2011

6. Bayley Stephen: Ugly, The Aesthetics of Everything (Overlook Hardcover 2013)

7. Cousins, Mark with Altar Hussain: The Ugly (London Macmillan 1984)

8. Cannadine, David: Ornamentalism and the Raj (History Today 2001 Issue 5, Vol. 51)

9. Ibid: Ornamentalism: How the British Saw Their Empire, (Allen Lane, London 2001)

10. Corinne, Julius: India's Maharajahs–The Best of Both Worlds (History Today 2009. Issue 10, Vol. 59)

11. Issue 10, Vol. 59

12. Cole, Mary E, The Politics of Heritage from Madras to Chennai: (Indiana University Press 2008)

13. Chattopadyay, Swati: Representing Calcutta: Modernity, Nationalism and the Colonial Uncanny, (Routledge Oxford, 2006)

14. Crinson, Mark: Orientalism & Victorian Architecture (Routledge Chapman & Hal, London 1996)

15. Dobbie, Aline The Elephant's Blessing (Melrose Books, Cambridgeshire, 2006)

16. Dufferin Papers: Our Viceregal Life in India (Letters from the Marquess of Dufferin and Ava, London, John Murray, 1889)

17. Eliot, Thomas S: The Wasteland and Other Poems (London, 1922)

18. Fergusson Niall: Empire (Penguin, Allen Lane, London 2003)

19. Gode Patrick The Jacobethan Style (Oxford Companion to Architecture) lover William J: Making Lahore Modern: Constructing and Imagining a Colonial City (University of Minnesota Press, Minneapolis and London, 2007)

20. Higman, Chris: Henry Irwin: Online biography by Higman consulting Gmbh

21. Keay John: A History of India (Harper Perrenial, London 2004)

22. .Kennedy Dane: The Magic Mountains (University of California Press, Berkeley 1996)

23. London Christopher: Bombay Gothic (Mumbai, India Book House Ltd. 2006)

24. Ibid: Architecture in Victorian and Edwardian India (Marg Publications Mumbai 1994)

25. Muthiah, S: Madras Rediscovered, Westland Ltd, Chennai, 1999

26. Mackenzie John: Victoria Terminus Bombay: History Today, 1989, Issue 1, Vol 29

27. Metcalf Thomas An Imperial Vision (University of California Press Berkeley 1989)

28. Ibid: Forging the Raj: (Oxford University Press, 2005)

29. Nangia Ashish:The History of Indian Architecture (Gsus79, 2012)

30. Sen Siddhartha: Architecture and Urban Planning Practices in Colonial India (School of Architecture and Planning, Morgan State University, Baltimore MD)

31. Sriram, V: Thattikonda Namberumal Chetty and Henry Irwin (Madras Heritage and Carnatic Music, 2012)

32. Stancliffe David: The Lion companion to Church Architecture (Lion Hudson, 2008)

33. Scriver, Peter ed. With Vikramaditya Prakash: Colonial Modernities–Building, Dwellings and Architecture in British India: (Routledge, Oxford, 2008)

34. Tillotson, GHR: Orientalising the Raj: Indo Saracenic Fantasies (Marg September 1994 Vol 46)

35. Tindall, Gillian: City of Gold (Penguin 1982)

36. Whiffen, Marcus: An Introduction to Elizabethan & Jacobean Architecture (Art and Technics London 1952)

37. Zeynek Celik: Colonialism, Orientalism & the Canon: The Art Bulletin (Vol. 78 Nbr 2 June 1986)

REVIEWS OF THE AUTHOR'S PREVIOUS BOOK "COLONIAL CALCUTTA: RELIGIOUS ARCHITECTURE AS A MIRROR OF EMPIRE" (BLOOMSBURY, 2012)

Critical acclaim for the writer's previous book, "Colonial Calcutta: Religious Architecture as a Mirror of Empire" (Bloomsbury 2012):

The Hindu, Chennai 15.3.2013

The book demystifies conventional ideas about Colonial Calcutta's religious architecture . . . The author focusses on British apathy towards other foreign immigrant communities and illustrates how even the indigenous religious architectural traditions of Bengal were influenced by a kind of Anglo Indian neo classicism handed down by East India Company engineers.

The Telegraph, Kolkata, 24.3.'2013

Pradip Das pleads his case in the Introduction: "This book is not a eulogy to the Raj nor is it written in a fit of elegiac nostalgia . . ." He shows that it (The Raj legacy) is not as glorious as it is made out to be and argues that Calcutta's Christian architecture designed to wean the native population from their own religious beliefs was often second rate . . ."

Prof. Tapan Raychaudhuri Emeritus Professor of Indian History, Oxford University

A brilliant synopsis of a complex subject,

Prof. Barun De, Tagore National Fellow, Former Chairman, West Bengal Heritage Commission 23.11.2013

Pradip Das's book reminds one of the affectionate work done on this city by amateur historians of the Bengal Past and Present tradition such as Sir Henry Evan Cotton . . . and the well known "Statesman" columnist, Desmond Doig. The book is a welcome tribute to some examples of the architecture of faith

Prof. S. Bhattacharya, Tagore National Fellow & Former Vice Chancellor, Vishwabharati University

A truly remarkable book . . . Calcutta deserved a well researched and beautifully illustrated book like this to guide citizens' attention to the temples, churches, mosques, synagogues and funerary monuments many of which languish in neglect . . ."

Carolyn and Martin Karcher, Washington DC USA, February 2013

A splendid book on religious architecture in Colonial Calcutta. The format is stunning and so are the pictures . . a prodigious piece of research.